T0289458

Competitive Strategy and Leadership

Competitive Strategy and Leadership

A Guide to Superior Performance

WILLIAM G. FORGANG

ROWMAN & LITTLEFIELD PUBLISHERS, INC.
Lanham • Boulder • New York • Oxford

ROWMAN & LITTLEFIELD PUBLISHERS, INC.

Published in the United States of America
by Rowman & Littlefield Publishers, Inc.
4720 Boston Way, Lanham, Maryland 20706
www.rowmanlittlefield.com

12 Hid's Copse Road
Cumnor Hill, Oxford OX2 9JJ, England

British Library Cataloguing in Publication Information Available

Library of Congress Cataloging-in-Publication Data

Forgang, William G., 1946–
    Competitive strategy and leadership : a guide to superior performance / William G. Forgang.
        p. cm.
    Includes bibliographical references and index.
    ISBN 0-7425-1279-7 (alk. paper)—ISBN 0-7425-1280-0 (pbk. : alk. paper)
    1. Strategic planning. 2. Leadership. I. Title.

    HD30.28 .F677 2001
    658.4'012—dc21

                                                                            2001019744

Printed in the United States of America

∞™ The paper used in this publication meets the minimum requirements of American National Standard for Information Sciences—Permanence of Paper for Printed Library Materials, ANSI/NISO Z39.48-1992.

Contents

Preface   vii

Acknowledgments   ix

Introduction   1

Preassessment Exercises   5
   Part 1: Memo   6
   Part 2: Self-Assessment   8

Case Study: The Gibsonville Lantern Company   9

1   *The Cycle of Success*   15
   • *The Cycle of Success*   16
   • Leadership and *The Cycle of Success*   30
   • Case Study: Gregory's Retirement Home Services   32

2   The Value Equation and the Nature of Services   35
   • The Value Equation   36
   • The Nature of Services   44
   • Value and Performance Measures: The Firm   46
   • Value and Performance Measures: The Individual   49

3   Strategy and Value Creation   53
   • Strategy and Mission   53
   • Mission, Strategy, and the Firm's Value Proposition   56
   • Line of Business and Corporate Strategies   65

4   Integrated Decisions, Operations, and Strategy   71
   • Strategy and Operating Areas   71
   • Strategy and the Connections among Operating Areas   79
   • Assessment of the Shift in Strategy at Gibsonville   83
   • Corporate-Level Strategies   83

5   Personal and Staff Attributes   87
    • Leadership and the Human Resource   87
    • Strategy, Skills, and Attributes   88
    • Strategy, Leadership, and Motivation   90
    • Building an Organizational Culture   94
    • Corporate-Level Strategies   99

6   Leading by Measurement System   103
    • Managing by Performance Measures   103

7   Leadership and *The Cycle of Success*   115
    • *The Cycle of Success*   115
    • Qualities of Strategic Leaders   116
    • Leaders and Managers   118
    • Leadership and Situational Analysis   119

Appendix
    • Postassessments   125
      Part 1: Memo   125
      Part 2: Self-Assessment   126
    • Facilitator's Guide to the Exercises   129

Index   141

About the Author   143

Preface

This book is directed toward those who want to win! Those who want their firm to be acknowledged as superior, those who seek financial rewards, those who seek the joys of association with winners, and those who accept responsibility for contributing to the success of their organization are sought as readers!

This book seeks to develop *winning organizations* through *strategic leaders*! *Winning organizations*

- excel at serving their buyers,
- outperform their rivals,
- offer a workplace environment that promotes winning attitudes and success, and
- realize favorable interactions between buyer and employee loyalty by *doing the right things correctly.*

Strategic leaders

- contribute to the design of a competitive strategy that provides their firm with a winning formula,
- implement strategy-specific operating policies and practices and effectively execute the firm's competitive strategy,
- manage by competitive theme and build a coherent organization,
- develop a management team and organizational culture around a common competitive theme,
- motivate coworkers by aligning each individual's duties and responsibilities with the firm's competitive strategy,
- monitor and communicate the execution of the firm's competitive strategy through carefully selected performance measurements, and
- make decisions in accord with the firm's strategy, building an organization that makes sense to buyers and employees, and win!

The conceptual model on which this book is built is termed *The Cycle of Success*. This model is intended to create superior performance for the firm, the individual, and each coworker, and

> *the simultaneous successes are the result of the implementation of a competitive strategy that meets buyer expectations, delivered through a set of strategy-specific operations, by individuals who possess the requisite skills and attributes.*

Winning organizations result from a wisely crafted competitive strategy and strategic leaders who properly align operating practices, tools, and people with that strategy. By carefully articulating their decision-making logic in terms of the firm's strategy, strategic leaders create a workplace environment that makes sense to employees. Everyone knows why decisions are made, and everyone knows their responsibilities and contributions to success. Winning occurs because buyers are served as intended by the firm's strategy, and the firm's employees enjoy the commonly directed efforts of their colleagues.

This book is not an easy read. It is not intended for those who seek a "quick fix" solution to management problems. Rather, it seeks to provide an integrated methodology for analyzing a firm's competitive strategy and shaping every employee's daily tasks. Those readers who succeed in capturing the holistic approach of this book are prepared to contribute to winning.

This book allows senior managers to become more effective by guiding their team through the formulation and implementation of the firm's strategy. Mid-level managers can be more effective by making decisions and recommendations within the context of their firm's strategy. Individual employees can improve their job performance by aligning their decisions, behavior, and professional development with their firm's strategy, and student readers can become better prepared to enter the world of work by understanding their initial duties in the context of their firm's strategy.

Acknowledgments

Many of the ideas expressed in this book are the result of a two-year leadership training program (LTP) that I facilitated on behalf of McLean, Koehler, Sparks & Hammond, a Maryland-based public accounting firm. I am grateful to the partners of the firm for allowing me to work with their managers and appreciative of the goodwill and challenging learning environment created by the LTP participants.

Several Mount Saint Mary's College (Emmitsburg, Maryland) colleagues provided a good deal of assistance, particularly Drs. D. Stephen Rockwood, John Hook, and Charles Beitz.

My wife, Nancy, provided valuable editorial assistance and encouragement. My writing could not have been completed without her support and faith.

Special thanks go to the editorial staff at the Rowman & Littlefield Publishing Group. Their promptness, courtesies, and guidance are greatly appreciated.

Introduction

This book develops a holistic approach for business decision making and for guiding professional development. The approach joins the rigors of strategic planning with the abstractions of leadership.

Successful readers will be better able to

- assess strategic opportunities and guide strategic planning for their firm,
- make decisions in accord with the requirements of conducting the firm's strategic plan,
- build a management team that understands and consistently executes the firm's strategy,
- recognize the tools, technologies, and skills necessary to implement the firm's strategy,
- establish a personal development plan and a human resources plan aligned with the firm's competitive strategy,
- build and monitor a set of performance measures that communicate the firm's strategy and monitor its implementation, and
- translate the firm's strategy into a motivating force, earning a strategy-based leadership role in the organization.

The primary topics of this book are business strategy and leadership. Among the many lessons in the following pages are that (1) these concerns cannot be confined within the ranks of senior management, (2) decision making throughout the firm must be aligned with the strategic plan, and (3) strategic leadership must exist at all levels of the firm.

An organization benefits from a clear competitive strategy, and this book helps individuals shape and articulate the manner in which their firm seeks to gain a competitive advantage over rivals. Because the implementation of the strategy requires the contribution of employees throughout the firm, all workers must understand the firm's strategy and act on the connections between their tasks and the requisites of conducting that strategy. As a result, the audience for this book should come from all levels of the firm, and maximum organizational benefits may result when a team of coworkers reads this book and completes the exercises at the same time under the direction of a trained facilitator.

To assist readers, this book includes several pedagogical features:

- Self-assessment exercises are completed *before* and *after* reading the book, serving as a means to document changes in the reader's thinking.
- A case study, the Gibsonville Lantern Company, is offered at the start of the book and is referred to throughout in textboxes. The Gibsonville Lantern case is used to highlight many of the key messages within the book.
- Exercises appear throughout the book. Readers are encouraged to write down and discuss their replies. In a classroom setting, the exercises may be used as homework assignments, and readers should not limit their replies to the spaces provided in the book.
- A second case study, Gregory's Retirement Home Services, is introduced at the end of chapter 1, and each chapter includes related exercises. The compilation of these Gregory's Retirement Home Services exercises may be used as a capstone assignment for a course in strategic planning or business policy.
- A guide to the exercises provides direction for completing the exercises and facilitating discussion.

This book may be used within a corporate training program and may be particularly beneficial when studied immediately prior to a firm's annual strategic planning cycle. The firm that seeks to build a more cohesive management team may use this book as a training exercise, and the principles developed in this book are equally applicable in for-profit and not-for-profit organizations. Those firms that employ large numbers of technically trained individuals (certified public accountants, engineers, researchers, etc.) may use the book to develop business skills, build a management team, strengthen consulting skills, build strategic leadership skills, and build a succession plan.

This book may also be used in a classroom setting as an alternative to the cumbersome undergraduate and M.B.A.-level strategic planning texts. It differs from traditional texts through (1) the emphasis on the *implementation* of a firm's strategic plan, (2) the analysis of the linkages between each operation and the firm's strategy, (3) the reflection on the importance of incorporating this strategy into the actions of all workers, and (4) the efforts to link the literatures of business strategy and leadership. When this book is used in an undergraduate or M.B.A.-level policy or strategy course, the *Balanced Corporate Scorecard* simulation (Harvard Business School Press, 1998) is a valuable supplement. Instructors may take advantage of the relative brevity of this book and use their favorite case studies to highlight key instructional themes. Furthermore, the emphasis on implementing the firm's strategy through the strategy-specific design of operations, policies, and procedures provides a framework for new graduates to understand their workplace responsibilities.

The reader is challenged to work through the volume carefully. Take each exercise seriously. Each one, separately, is less than crucial, but the total learning opportunity is greater than the sum of the parts. As in the professional service setting, each contact with a client or prospective client may seem small and inconsequential, yet the sum of those small and seemingly inconsequential contacts is the foundation of the service provider's reputation and competitive strength. This is similarly true of the following exercises. Think carefully about each piece; the total learning is a leveraged product of the commitment to the small pieces.

Preassessment Exercises

There are two "preassessment exercises" to be completed *prior* to reading this book. These preassessment exercises provide baseline measures of the reader's abilities and confidence in strategic management. Upon completion of the book, the reader is advised to repeat the assessment exercises and reflect on the changes in his or her replies. In a business environment, the pre- and postassessments may reflect the development of a cohesive management team. In a classroom setting, the pre- and postassessments may help the instructor evaluate the learning outcomes of the course.

The preassessment exercises appear on the following pages.

PART 1: MEMO

Assume you have been charged to develop a new profit center within your organization, perhaps involving the introduction of a new product or service. Or you may have been assigned the task of developing a new set of procedures to reengineer current operations. *For students who do not have an employer as a point of reference, use your campus as an example. Consider the possible expansion of the Student Union or Career Center, the development of a new major program, or the allocation of scholarship monies to high academic achievers, athletes, selected minorities, or some other precisely defined group.*

You have the opportunity to select the team that will complete the analytical work, and the size of your team is not limited. You are responsible for the project and for leading the team members' study.

In the space below, guide their work, noting that they will provide only that information specifically requested. You are not to write a business plan. Do not preempt the work of your team members. Rather, shape their analysis through detailed instructions. Do not limit your reply to the space provided on page 7.

Step #1:

    State the premise:

_____

_____

Step #2:

    Write the memo:

To: _____

From: _____

Re: _____

Date: _____

PART 2: SELF-ASSESSMENT

Reply to the following, using a scale of 1 to 10 (1 = low, 10 = high), expressing your confidence with each of the assignments. *Students should reply from the perspective of their current capabilities and as if in their first job.*

Score	Assignment
	You have been asked to be part of a team to develop a strategic plan for your firm.
	You have been asked to lead a team to develop a strategic plan for your firm.
	You have been asked to develop a mentoring system for new junior-level employees.
	You have been asked to develop and implement a staff evaluation system.
	You have been asked to make recommendations to correct a morale problem.
	You have been asked to define criteria for making an important hiring decision.
	You have been asked to evaluate the level of customer service extended by your firm.
	You have been asked to develop a plan to coordinate decisions among departments in your firm.
	You have been asked to define the skills and attributes to become a vice president in your firm.
	You have been asked to define ways in which buyers evaluate your firm's performance.
	You have been asked to develop an in-house seminar on motivation.
	You have been asked to evaluate your firm's hiring procedures.
	You have been asked to evaluate the leadership in your firm.
	You have been asked to develop a means to assess the broad business skills of colleagues or prospective employees.
	You have been asked to mediate differences of opinion on an important policy issue in your firm.
	You have been asked to develop a plan to distribute end-of-year bonuses or merit raises.
	You have been asked to define the manner in which your firm tries to gain a competitive advantage over rivals.
	You have been asked to develop an action plan to improve operating efficiencies in your firm.
	You have been asked to evaluate the organizational structure in your firm.
	You have been asked to write a personal growth plan.

Case Study: The Gibsonville Lantern Company

Please read the case before proceeding:

1. Exercises throughout the book refer to this case.
2. "Textbox" information highlights concepts through references to this case.
3. Readers are encouraged to draft a memo in reply to this case, writing to Mr. Barker Jr. and to Mr. Landis. Provide specific advice.

Upon completion of the book, review these memos and reflect on how you would write them differently.

The Gibsonville Lantern Company

John Landis, vice president for Sales for the Gibsonville Lantern Company, is seated at his desk on a Sunday afternoon, trying to prepare for his first formal presentation to the company president, Ted Barker Jr. Although he was appointed to the vice presidential position only two months ago, the brief period has been traumatic for him and the company. Sales and new orders have tumbled nearly 8 percent, accelerating the decline of the prior two years. While some decline had been expected as a result of a shift in competitive strategy, the slump has been greater than expected. Further, the recent results indicate that conditions are getting worse rather than better, and this is particularly troublesome given the strength of the economy and the boom in construction spending.

Though fully aware of the importance of identifying the cause of the current downturn and of drafting a marketing plan, John is finding it difficult to prepare for this important meeting. Crises seem to arise on a daily basis, each demanding his immediate attention. Further, because many of these crises involve long-term clients and employees, John anticipates that Ted Barker Jr. will ask specific questions about how such situations are being handled. As stress levels mount, John is eager to seize the opportunity to help the company reverse its recent fortunes and to solidify his position as a vice president.

Company History

Ted Barker Sr., seventy-eight, founded the Gibsonville Lantern Company in 1946 upon returning home after military service. He gained his foundry and pattern-making skills while serving on naval bases during the war. He started the company in his basement, initially making gift items. As the business grew, he cautiously moved into larger manufacturing facilities and specialized in exterior lighting fixtures. Though business proved to be vulnerable to energy price shocks and sensitive to peaks and troughs in residential and commercial construction, low debt and tight cost controls helped the company endure. Ted Barker Sr. has remarked that "over the years, the business has been good to me and my family. Though there have been struggles at times, I am proud to have built this business, and it continues to meet the economic needs of my family."

In the very early years, the company operated out of the basement and garage of the Barker home and produced customized items including railings, lampposts, lanterns, and other decorative metal products. The customization of the products meant that few items were produced before an order was received.

As the business grew, the home-based facilities proved to be too small. In 1954, Ted Barker Sr. made the decision to move to larger facilities and to assume the risk of growing the business. Barker made the decision to borrow from the local bank, promising that this would be a one-time use of external funds. The 1954 facility necessitated longer production runs to achieve efficiencies. Over time, the Gibsonville Lantern Company gravitated toward producing a small number of different products, involving very traditional designs. Redesign and customization added considerable expense. Sales reps carried with them product samples, and local retailers maintained modest inventories. The commission-based reps visited retailers periodically to monitor and replenish inventories. Retailers acknowledge that the Gibsonville products have always been solid, fully functional, dependable, and modestly priced. At the foundry, Gibsonville tried to operate at a nearly steady production rate, reflecting Barker's commitment to providing stable employment to his workforce. Still, production did vary as dictated by the seasonal and cyclical sensitivity of sales.

In addition to expanding the foundry capabilities in 1954, Ted Barker Sr. recognized the need to increase the geographic scope of their sales and the size of the sales force. The existing distribution network was insufficient to generate the volume of business needed to make the new foundry profitable. The sales force expansion increased the number of fully commission-based reps who served small and mid-sized town hardware stores and lumberyards. The Gibsonville reps did not work exclusively for Barker. Generally, they represented several noncompeting firms, offering a variety of hardware and related product. Given the nontechnical nature of Gibsonville's products, there were no particular product knowledge demands placed on the reps. Though they needed to be comfortable within the local hardware store and lumberyard markets, the primary demands were to maintain honorable relationships with retailers and to replenish inventory several times per year.

In the early 1990s, Gibsonville began to struggle. Despite cost-cutting initiatives and price reductions, the difficulties intensified. The product mix was old and tired. The traditional retail vendors—neighborhood hardware stores and lumberyards—were declining in number and in importance for builders and home remodelers. Large discount retail stores and mass market building supply/home stores were gaining market share, and Gibsonville's modest size prevented it from penetrating these distribution channels.

In 1999, Ted Sr.—suffering from bad health—turned the business over to his eldest son. Ted Jr. understood the market circumstances challenging Gibsonville. Three months after taking over the firm, Ted Jr. announced his decision to move the company back to its roots, producing highly styled, custom products.

John Landis

As John sits at his desk to prepare his presentation, he first sorts the phone and e-mail messages of the prior week. He knows Ted Barker Jr. will ask about the hot issues. While concerned about the immediate problems, John is uneasy about the firm's transition from the old to the new strategy.

The messages, compiled by John Landis's secretary are as follows:

- Graphicscom Printing: Called a third time in two days, wanting to know the final price figures so our catalog can be printed. Any further delays will result in the catalog being bumped from the production schedule causing a delay in delivery of several weeks.
- Schmidt's Hardware: Called again, complaining about (our rep) Bob Johnson. . . . Says Johnson is useless. . . . We have trouble getting in touch with him. . . . When we do, he never knows the answers to our questions about price, availability, or delivery time. Karl Schmidt seems serious. He threatened to stop doing business with us if the situation does not improve.
- Richard Chen: Says he is about to quit, despite many years representing our company. Says he places orders and products are not shipped on time, resulting in disgruntled customers. Says many of the other reps he talks to are unhappy. Quotas have not changed, commission checks are shrinking, and old accounts are being lost even as the reps continue to do what has always been successful.
- Steve Rockwell: I am trying to make a major sale to a housing developer. The development project is 150 upscale homes, involving front and rear exterior lights, doorknockers, decorative items, and porch and patio railings. But I can't answer the technical questions. The sales materials are inadequate, and I can't get through to the production staff. We are going to lose this sale—and it will not be my fault!
- Elgardo Rodriguez: Urgent: your reps are promising delivery that we in Production can't meet!!! Get some control over your staff! You are in charge. Fix things!

- Tom Ryan: Just a reminder that next Friday is my last day; as yet, I have not heard if you have hired a replacement for me. But next week is the last chance for me to train and introduce the new rep to my territory and my most important retail outlets.
- Zerling's Hardware: We are closing at the end of next month, unable to keep going. Wal-Mart and Home Depot have done us in. Our fifty years together have been a pleasure, and I wish you success. I am eager to return your unsold merchandise; please ask Abby Johns—your rep—to pick up the approximately two dozen pieces.

John Landis, looking at the sales data, sees that almost all territories are reporting declines. He knows it is necessary to develop a marketing and sales strategy. But everything seems to be out of control. Accounts are being lost, routine materials are not being developed, and the reps are rebelling.

Note

The Gibsonville Lantern case borrows several important themes from a Darden School, University of Virginia, case study: Battlefield Furniture.

In the spaces below, note your specific recommendations to Ted Barker Jr. and to John Landis.

To: Ted Barker Jr.

Re: _____

_____

_____

_____

_____

_____

_____

_____

_____

To: John Landis

Re: _____

_____

_____

_____

_____

_____

_____

_____

_____

CHAPTER 1

The Cycle of Success

This book is intended to foster success for the firm, for you, and for your coworkers. The management model developed throughout this book, *The Cycle of Success,* builds a holistic view of the firm through which the firm's competitive strategy is analyzed and implemented. As a guide for current and future managers, *The Cycle of Success* provides a means to formulate a firm's competitive approach to market and to select from alternative operating practices, policies, equipment, budget allocations, and personnel. As a guide to decision making, *The Cycle of Success* builds strategic leaders at all levels of the firm.

The Cycle of Success proposes that superior performance results from merging several themes. See table 1.1.

Table 1.1.   Contributors to Superior Performance

- Leadership skills that breed achievement, worker loyalty, and buyer satisfaction
- Reliance on strategy-specific performance measures to communicate and monitor the implementation of the firm's strategy
- Strategy-specific operating policies and practices
- The particular combination of product features, service, and price that the firm sells and which serve buyer needs

The simultaneous achievement of the four items listed in the table is the basis of a successfully executed strategy that (1) serves buyers and earns their loyalty and (2) provides satisfying work experiences for employees and earns their loyalty. The favorable interactions between strategy and operations and buyer and employer loyalty coincides with the realization of superior performance.

Before proceeding, two points must be stressed:

1. *A Means of Analysis:* Because the subject of this book is extremely broad, it is not possible to exhaust any individual topic. Rather than attempting thoroughness on any specific topic, this book builds a methodology. *The Cycle of Success* offers a holistic model of the firm, linking the firm's competitive strategy to the satisfaction of buyer expectations and to the design of its internal operating systems and practices.

The model is extended to a human resource plan, a personal development plan, and a means to build leadership skills at all levels of the organization.

2. *A Process, Not an End Solution:* The methodology offered throughout this book is a process. There is no simple means to impose the system on a firm. It is improper to think that either the system exists in a firm or does not so exist. Rather, a firm experiences degrees of compliance with the methodology. There is no end point, but firms and individuals—as a result of their own choices—may move closer or farther away from reaping the benefits of the model.

The Cycle of Success reflects a series of entwined ideas that evolve over time, and the reader is likely to ponder how such a system can be implemented. Unfortunately, no simple answer exists. However, understanding the model is the first step toward implementation, and the exercises throughout the book are a means to practice strategy-based decision making. Superior returns are more likely to accrue to those firms that implement practices that abide by the methodology. In contrast, some firms and individuals may be unable to think holistically and may remain continuously mired in details and unable to see connections between bits of data. Other firms may lack the ability to sustain a commitment to a belief system, always responding instead to the pressures of daily events and crises. For these firms, the long run prognosis is not good.

The Cycle of Success

In this opening chapter, *The Cycle of Success* is summarized, and the chapters that follow will examine specific subjects in greater detail. *The Cycle of Success* (see figure 1.1) is made up of interdependent triangles representing the firm, you, and your coworkers. The resultant fourth and central triangle, superior performance, is the outcome of the successful integration of the other three. The model is easily understood by examining its components.

Figure 1.1. *The Cycle of Success*

TRIANGLE #1: THE FIRM

The top triangle in *The Cycle of Success* refers to the firm (see figure 1.2). The starting point is buyer expectations. Buyers seek to maximize their well-being, given their finite incomes. For each purchase, buyers seek the most favorable ratio of benefits to costs. Benefits include the tangible and intangible results of buying the good or service *plus* the ease, convenience, and confidence in the item purchased. The costs include the purchase price, ongoing operating and maintenance expenses, plus any unpleasantries, inconveniences, and uncertainties associated with making the purchase. The ratio of benefits to costs is referred to as the *value proposition.*[1]

Figure 1.2.   Triangle #1: The Firm

The *buyer's value proposition* (see figure 1.3) includes distinct components: results, process quality (the favorable experiences associated with completing the transaction), price, and the cost of acquisition (the negative aspects of completing the transaction). Each buyer enters into the marketplace with different tastes and preferences. One buyer may be particularly price conscious, whereas another may seek specific product features, and another may be very sensitive to the convenience of the transaction and to after-purchase service.

$$\textbf{Value} = \frac{Results + Process\ Quality}{Price + Cost\ of\ Acquisition}$$

Figure 1.3.   Value Proposition

Table 1.2 reflects a hypothetical automobile purchaser's value proposition. While it is unlikely that any buyers would actually write down their value proposition in this form, the actual buying choice reflects the weighted mix of their aspirations. For the hypothetical buyer depicted in table 1.2, the purchase price is relatively unimportant, though it must be perceived as "fair." Prestige, appearance, performance, and the resale value are concerns.

Connected to buyer expectations in *The Cycle of Success* is the firm's competitive strategy, the means through which a firm gains a price or product advantage over rivals and earns superior returns. A well-conceived competitive strategy yields

Table 1.2.   Hypothetical Buyer's Value Proposition: Automobile Purchase

Value Factors	Percentage of Weight Given to Each Factor	
Result	60	
Miles per gallon		0
Safety		10
Seating capacity		5
Prestige and appearance		30
Performance		55
Subtotal		100
Process Quality	25	
Courtesy of sales staff		55
Absence of selling pressures		15
Sense of getting a vehicle at proper price		30
Subtotal		100
Price	10	
Price inclusive of rebates and discounts		20
Operating and maintenance expenses		10
Resale value		70
Subtotal		100
Cost of Acquisition	5	
Price haggling		0
Comparison shopping (time and expense)		50
Sense of not having negotiated the best deal		50
Subtotal		100
Total	100	

a *seller's value proposition,* which is different from that of rivals and which serves targeted buyers in important ways. A competitive advantage is achieved through a particular weighted mix of variables in the value proposition that meshes with the aspirations of *targeted* buyers, thereby providing them with their most favorable ratio of benefits to costs.

The strength of the firm's competitive strategy (see table 1.3) is determined by the buyers based on the attractiveness of the firm's value proposition relative to that of makers of rival products, the extent to which the product can be replicated by competitors, and the degree to which the firm effectively delivers its value proposition.

Table 1.3 provides a means through which the firm can assess the potential profitability of its strategy. However, winning organizations possess more than a

Table 1.3.   Strength of Competitive Advantage

- The ability of rivals to replicate the firm's value proposition
- The ability of the firm to sustain its effective delivery of the value proposition over time
- The difference between a firm's value proposition and that of rival sellers
- The effectiveness of the firm's execution of its value proposition
- The firm's ability to adapt to changing market conditions
- The importance of that difference to buyers
- The size and affluence of the targeted buyer group

good idea for their business. A good concept is not enough! Table 1.3 also indicates that the best conceived strategies must be effectively implemented, raising issues of internal operations, the third leg of triangle #1. *The Cycle of Success argues that each operation within the firm must be designed in accord with the requisites of delivering the seller's value proposition.*

Triangle #1 in *The Cycle of Success* seeks a confluence among buyer expectations, the firm's strategy, and the design of its internal operations. Seven important ideas emerge from triangle #1:

1. Type I Buyers
2. Designing Activities
3. Rigidity of the Value Proposition
4. Linking Activities
5. Managing by Theme
6. Benchmarking
7. Decision Making

Gibsonville Lantern

The case describes the transition of the firm from selling high-volume, low-margin, and standardized products to producing high-margin, customized products. With the change in the firm's competitive strategy, the firm must identify its new target buyers and build new distribution channels.

Type I Buyers

Not all buyers are equally attractive to a firm. Firms can make egregious errors by failing to identify their target buyers and the particular weighted mix of variables that constitute value for their target buyers. Mismatches between the seller's value proposition and that of buyers have serious negative effects, including low buyer satisfaction, low rates of repeat purchase, and poor word-of-mouth promotion. Furthermore, it may be costly for a firm to serve a "mismatched" buyer (see table 1.4). For example, a manufacturer that produces a standardized and commodity-like product may find it awkward to serve a buyer who demands customization. In addition to the added engineering costs, personnel and production systems may be ill-equipped for short runs of unique products. In addition to imposing high costs on the seller, the mismatched buyer may be quick to turn to a rival seller that has a greater ability to operate in a job-shop manner.

Table 1.4.   Costs of New Buyers

- New buyers do not know the seller's procedures and require more guidance from frontline personnel
- New buyers must be carefully nurtured as a relationship is built
- New buyers require the seller to learn their unique needs

Firms can reap significant benefits by estimating and analyzing their "Quality Buyer Ratio," which is the proportion of Type I to "Total" Buyers (see figure 1.4). Type I Buyers are those whose value proposition is closely meshed with the seller's, and the Quality Buyer Ratio may be a leading indicator of the firm's success. The firm with a predominance of Type I Buyers enjoys the luxury of repeat purchases, favorable word-of-mouth promotion, and the avoidance of the costs associated with mismatched buyers.

$$\textbf{Quality Buyer Ratio} = \frac{Type\ I\ Buyers}{Total\ Buyers}$$

Figure 1.4.   Quality Buyer Ratio

There is no single target value for this ratio; it varies between firms and industries for many reasons. Differences in the maturity of a firm, the intensity of the competitiveness in the industry, and the rate of technical change can affect a firm's Quality Buyer Ratio. However, a higher ratio is preferred to a lower one, and firms should seek to improve their ratios. *Because sales are not equally attractive to the seller, marketing efforts, commissions, and other rewards to employees should be based on the attractiveness of a new account.*

Exercise 1.1

Define Type I Buyers for your firm in the context of the value proposition. Estimate the ratio of Type I to Total Buyers. Finally, write a brief Action Plan to raise the proportion of Type I Buyers. For students, select any firm with which you are familiar (perhaps your school) to complete the following.

Firm: _____

Type I Buyers: _____

_____

_____

Percentage of Type I Buyers to Total Buyers: _____ %

Action Plan: _____

_____

_____

(The reader is referred to the Facilitator's Guide—pages 129–40—for assistance with the exercises.)

Designing Activities

Integrated operations represent the third leg of triangle #1 in *The Cycle of Success,* and the focus is on the implementation of the seller's value proposition. The price, results, process quality, or acquisition cost advantages are the outcome of distinct "activities." In the language of Michael Porter, a firm gains a competitive advantage over rivals by performing similar activities differently or by performing different activities.[2] *In sum, the value proposition should be delivered through a set of strategy-specific operations—physical, human, technological, and cultural.*

Gibsonville Lantern

When the firm switched from standardized mass produced products to customized products, many individual processes needed to be changed. For example, the new strategy forced Manufacturing from an assembly line format focused on long production runs and low unit costs to a job shop to accommodate the demands of customization. *The design of individual activities is dictated by the nature of the firm's strategy.*

For example, a men's fine clothing store should select a location, decor, inventory, tailoring, and sales personnel in accord with the requisites of the execution value of its value proposition. These individual activities should be different from those at a discount clothier. Similarly, a bakery that prides itself on high-end and fresh goods should design menu items, procurement practices, ovens and other tools, work schedules, inventory management, and delivery schedules in accord with its value proposition, and these will differ from analogous activities at a bakery that focuses on price and length of shelf life. *The appropriate way "to do things" can only be determined by the requisites of implementing the value proposition.*

Rigidity of the Value Proposition

As discussed, a firm's competitive strategy is based on finding a particular weighted mix of variables in its value proposition. In turn, the specific operations within the firm should be designed in accord with the requisites of implementing the value proposition. Table 1.5 identifies selected activities for a restaurant.

Table 1.5.   Selected Activities: A Restaurant

• Exterior design	• Menu items
• Food buying	• Personnel selection
• Food preparation	• Pricing
• Interior décor	• Serving style
• Kitchen tools	• Tables/utensils
• Location	• Training

Noting that the design of these activities should be strategy specific, a fast food restaurant designs its menu, cooking, and serving operations differently from a fine dining establishment. Importantly, once the firm designs its activities, its flexibility is reduced. The restaurant that competes on the basis of fine food served elegantly lacks the production tools and work systems to satisfy those buyers who want a meal served quickly. Trying to serve the two market segments (fast and elegant) at the same time may be problematic. A restaurant may be good at one or the other but not both at the same time. While efforts to design flexible systems can sometimes be appropriate, efforts to finesse systems to serve the two sets of buyers may undermine the firm's competitive strength.

Firms that try to serve diverse buyers at the same time risk confusing their employees. A chef may become uncertain in decision making by sometimes choosing recipes, food preparation procedures, and equipment based on elegance and other times choosing those based on quick service. The outcomes may be (1) mismatched decisions and a poorly executed value proposition and (2) a chef who exhibits low morale, poor productivity, and quickly seeks more professionally satisfying employment elsewhere. The threat of a poorly designed and executed value proposition is serious. It may lead to dissatisfied buyers and to employees sensing a leadership vacuum because decisions appear to be random and arbitrary. *In contrast, winning organizations create a set of internal operating decisions that make sense because they stem from the coherent execution of a competitive strategy.*

A caution is offered: *Don't "straddle!"*[3] The concept of straddling markets refers to a seller's attempt to serve different buyer segments with different value propositions with a single set of goods and production processes. The temptation to straddle is real. It appears to be a means to facilitate growth by capturing a new buyer or market segment. But firms must understand the limitations imposed by the design of their activities and serve only those buyers who can be satisfied within the constraints of the firm's tools, systems, processes, and capabilities.

Gibsonville Lantern

For Gibsonville Lantern, the success of the Sales Department is contingent on the proper support and coordination with Manufacturing and Shipping, and these departments are similarly dependent on other operating areas. Manufacturing's ability to customize products depends on the decisions made by Procurement. In turn, Procurement's success in securing timely delivery of unique inputs depends on the decisions made in Accounts Payable.

Linking Activities

While the firm must design its individual activities in accord with the value proposition, it must also manage the linkages between functional areas. For example, the effectiveness of a chef in a fine dining establishment is dependent on the restaurant's buyers to purchase high-quality and fresh foodstuffs, the tools and equipment in the kitchen, and the abilities of the serving personnel. If the linkages are not carefully managed, the firm's value proposition cannot be effectively delivered, making the firm less attractive to buyers.

The linkages between functional areas raise a host of very complex managerial issues. Functional area managers (perhaps in Marketing, Customer Service, Personnel, or Manufacturing) are dependent on the cooperation of peers who manage the other departments. The ability of a marketing manager for a motel chain to raise occupancy rates depends, in part, on the performance of the Housekeeping Department at each motel. Housekeeping operations, however, fall beyond the span of control of the marketing manager. In turn, Housekeeping is dependent on Procurement's selection of easy-to-clean carpets and furnishings and the quality of the cleaning materials. As a result, *the firm's organizational design, committee structure, cross-functional work teams, re-*

Gibsonville Lantern

For Gibsonville Lantern, the change in strategy alters the dependencies between departments. Under the old strategy, Sales and Manufacturing worked independently. Under the new strategy, they are closely dependent.

Senior-level managers must recognize the new linkages between departments and be sure that the organizational structure and reporting channels support these linkages. *In the absence of effectively managed interdepartmental linkages, the value proposition cannot be successfully implemented.*

porting relationships, and communication systems must serve the essential linkages between activities. Particular attention must be given to those linkages that cross managerial spans of control. Lines of authority must be carefully established, and formal procedures must be put in place to ensure the proper coordination. Performance standards and reward systems must be internally consistent and in compliance with the requisites of delivering the firm's competitive strategy.

Managing by Theme

The firm's intended value proposition creates a "management theme." The value proposition and its weighted mix of variables reflect that which is important in the firm's efforts to meet buyer expectations, and this theme should guide all practices and operating decisions in the firm. Two directives result:

• Be a Focused Value Provider/Manage by Theme!
• Do the Right Thing—Don't Just Do Things Right.

These challenges are significant. The firm's value proposition must be clear to employees, and firms must have the confidence and courage to do things differently than their rivals. How others do things is not necessarily right for us! *Different firms rightfully seek to offer different value propositions, and each firm must design its operations in accord with its value proposition.*[4]

Benchmarking

The firm that tries to assess its internal operations according to industry practices is engaged in potentially destructive behavior. Widespread benchmarking of processes to industry practices runs the risk of homogenizing one's goods or services by conforming to the value propositions of rivals.[5] Each firm's goods or services will increasingly resemble those of others, and interfirm rivalries will become priced based. Profits will decline for those sellers trapped in the commoditization of their goods or services, unless a firm is able to sustain a cost of production advantage.

Benchmarking is not inherently bad. Quite the contrary is true. Gaining information about rivals can be important. No firm would seek to be purposefully inefficient, and firms can learn from understanding "best practices," even if such practices are not adopted. Sometimes, lending institutions require a potential borrower to benchmark operations to industry averages. A firm seeking a loan may have to report, for example, the average number of days for its accounts receivable. The industry average—though informative—can be misleading. A particular firm may have an average collection period of fifty-five days compared with an industry average of forty days. But rival firms may have a credit policy that seeks payment in thirty days, whereas the firm in question may have "easy payment schedules" as a heavily weighted variable in its value proposition. This firm's credit policy may be sixty days. Benchmarking to the industry standard without regard to the firm's value proposition would provide misleading data to managers.

Gibsonville Lantern

With the change in strategy from standardized to customized products, the firm's performance standards must change. Under the old strategy, unit production costs may have been the most important, suggesting the importance of long production runs. Under the new strategy, design awards and timely deliveries are more important, and long production and lower unit costs become less important. A single set of benchmarked standards would not accurately reflect Gibsonville's performance under the old and new strategies.

An important point is that benchmarking may be business hygiene. Benchmarking can lead to operational efficiency in the context of the firm's strategy. But efficiencies can be replicated, and efficient operations—albeit important—are not a substitute for strategy unless the efficiencies are sustained and relative to rivals.[6] *Strategy involves building a price or product difference—expressed through the weighted mix of variables in the value proposition—that is important to buyers and is not easily replicated by rivals.*

Decision Making

As we become suspicious of benchmarking as a means to evaluate performance levels in a firm, we also want to become suspicious of some abstract sense of logic in making operating decisions. As we have all sat in committee meetings where different people argue abstractly for different actions, we want to become conscious of the appropriate standard by which to evaluate options. *How does a decision option relate to the delivery of our particular value proposition? Policy, procedure, budget allocation, and decision options should be assessed in terms of consistency with the delivery of the firm's value proposition.*

Often, it is revealing for a manager to reflect on differences of opinion expressed by colleagues or staff. In circumstances in which recommendations are markedly different, there may be valid differences in judgment. Such may be healthy. Organizations are well served by creative thinkers and healthful tensions. Still, close inspection of the differences of opinion is necessary to determine if there are underlying disagreements over the firm's value proposition or the definition of Type I Buyers. When significant disparities of opinion exist, the firm may be at risk because there is no consensus about the criteria by which decision options are evaluated. One must always fear the possibility that the organization lacks a common understanding of its value proposition.

For example, a bank may experience debate among employees about the appropriate hours of operation. Arguments may range from (1) more hours are costly and customers should use the ATMs or computer-based procedures to (2) our customers are personal service oriented and want to come into the bank to complete their transactions with tellers. Such differences of opinion in a single institution may be dangerous, reflecting disparities in employee belief systems about the seller's value proposition. The consequences may be an uncertain mix in hours of operation, service fees, size of staff, marketing themes, and the nature of employee–client interactions as some decisions are made based on efficiency in operations and others are driven by high touch service. Similarly, a private, nonprofit social service organization may experience internal debate over enforcing strict criteria for use of the services versus providing easy and dignified access. The lack of clarity may result in an internally inconsistent set of rules and practices and even inconsistent behaviors of employees over time.

Without a doubt, managers must evaluate decision options and assess tradeoffs. The bank president should see a tug-of-war between the desirability of preserving hours of service for convenience to depositors and the necessities of reducing labor costs. The choice may be a difficult one, and no single answer exists for all banks. The recommendations are to *(1) assess the decision options in terms of the effects on the firm's ability to deliver its value proposition and (2) examine differences of opinion to determine if valid competing positions exist or if the differences of opinion reflect an underlying disagreement over the firm's value proposition.*

Exercise 1.2

For your firm, Gibsonville Lantern, or a firm with which you are familiar, describe each of the three legs of the top triangle and evaluate their consistency.

Buyer Expectations: _____

_____

_____

Competitive Strategy: _____

_____

_____

Integrated Operations: _____

_____

_____

TRIANGLE #2: YOU!

The lower left triangle of *The Cycle of Success* (see figure 1.5) relates to you! One of the themes of this book is that the execution of the firm's strategy occurs through *all* individuals in the organization. We emphasize your particular status within the organization is unimportant. You may be a senior- or low-level manager or a functionary. But winning organizations have leaders at all levels, regardless of specific obligations.[7]

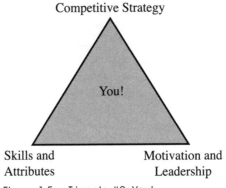

Figure 1.5.   Triangle #2: You!

The starting point of triangle #2 is the firm's competitive strategy and the explicit decision to deliver a particular weighted mix of variables in its value proposition. The first connection focused on in this triangle is the link between the firm's competitive strategy and the specific skills and attributes for each job. The human resource implications of *The Cycle of Success* are the subject of chapter 5. But it is important at this point to consider three ideas:

1. Required Skills and Attributes
2. Managing Human Resources
3. Tools and Equipment

Required Skills and Attributes

Individuals in different firms within an industry and serving in similar capacities may have nearly identical formal job descriptions. That does not, however, imply that individuals are interchangeable between firms. *Different seller value propositions imply different requisite skill and attribute mixes,* and a leader must have the courage to hire only those who are *just right for that firm!* For example, buyers for restaurants may have similar job descriptions, but the specific performance criteria will vary by the individual firm's strategy. Therefore, an individual suited for work with a fine dining establishment may be unhappy and ineffective completing similar functions for a fast food chain.

Part of the requisite skill and attribute mix is the individual employee's comfort and satisfaction level working within the confines of the firm's value proposition.[8] Importantly, the firm's value proposition and associated policies and procedures define the

Gibsonville Lantern

The strategy shift at Gibsonville Lantern creates a set of personnel problems, readily seen through the eyes of John Landis. The sales reps he inherited are associated with the old strategy of standardized products. The requisite skill and attribute set was defined by the demands of selling a commodity-like product through hardware stores and lumberyards.

The new strategy necessitates greater product knowledge. Also, the reps need selective personal skills and general knowledge to operate effectively in more sophisticated marketing channels. *The same person in the same job suddenly becomes ill-equipped, given the change in strategy.*

individual employee's work environment. For example, a physician who is properly trained and seeks to work in emergency medicine may be unhappy and unproductive in a family medicine practice. Similarly, a highly creative graphics artist may be uncomfortable and unhappy in a firm that produces routine, low-priced work under quick delivery schedules. No value judgments are implied, except to state that *the failure to align personnel skills and attributes with the dictates of the strategy weakens both employee loyalty and a firm's execution of its value proposition.*

Managing Human Resources

The skill and attribute mix demanded for the execution of the firm's strategy should become the basis on which new personnel are hired, the basis on which personnel are trained, and the basis of the firm's hiring, training, and compensation system. For example, the law firm that focuses on long-term relationships with clients may need a compensation system that places heavy weight on seniority, perhaps even at the expense of some relative weight assigned to billable hours. Similarly, because serving clients over long periods of time may necessitate offering many legal subspecialties, the law firm may limit the acceptable pay differentials between practice areas and build collegiality to improve client relationships. Because not all attorneys will be comfortable in this setting, the firm's hiring practices must clearly specify the environment and strategy-specific policies to avoid hiring mistakes. *No single set of human resource procedures makes sense across firms. Procedures, policies, and decisions must serve the execution of the firm's competitive strategy.*

Gibsonville Lantern

John Landis must reconsider the design of the operations in his area, including hiring, marketing channels, and training. The dictates of the new strategy are different from those of the old.

Landis must replace Tom Ryan, who is retiring, with an individual who fits the new strategy. The old hiring practices are unlikely to yield an appropriate replacement. Further, it is important for Landis to adapt the training, compensation, and reward systems to accommodate the demands of the new strategy.

Tools and Equipment

The skills and attributes of the human resource do not, by themselves, deliver the value proposition. The implementation of the competitive strategy depends on personnel being equipped with the necessary set of tools. *The tools and systems must contribute to extraordinary performance as opposed to expecting the extraordinary work of individuals to overcome inadequate tools.* The failure to adequately equip personnel to deliver the value proposition weakens the firm's competitiveness, and it also breeds employee disillusionment, lowers morale, and fosters turnover.

Gibsonville Lantern

Given the customization strategy of Gibsonville, it is important for the sales rep to keep in close contact with each client and be able to quickly secure information from Manufacturing and Shipping. To meet these new obligations, the reps need contemporary communications devices. These tools were not essential under the old strategy. Failure to provide the equipment may lead to ineffective execution of the value proposition and deteriorating morale among the reps.

Exercise 1.3

Describe the human resource practices in your firm or some firm with which you are familiar. Evaluate the consistency between these practices and the requisites of conducting the firm's value proposition.

_____

_____

_____

_____

_____

The third corner of the lower left triangle of *The Cycle of Success* relates to the individual's responsibility to build strategy-specific skills and attributes in others across the organization. The nature of an individual's influence may take several different forms and depends on the placement of the individual within the organization's hierarchy. While some individuals have the authority to establish hiring practices, set compensation and reward systems, coach/mentor, or discipline, everyone has some capability to communicate vertically and horizontally within the firm. Where well-executed "nagging" around the firm's strategy occurs,[9] a positive culture reinforces the delivery of the value proposition.

TRIANGLE #3: COWORKERS

The third triangle in *The Cycle of Success* refers to your coworkers, at all levels of the firm (see figure 1.6). The starting point is the upper corner, integrated operations. The implementation of the firm's competitive strategy dictates that individual activities be designed in accord with the requisites of delivering the value proposition. The nature of individual operations, operating policies, and practices is strategy specific. *In turn, motivation and strategic leadership responsibilities include building an organizational culture within which all decisions are aligned with the firm's value proposition.*

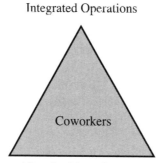

Integrated Operations

Coworkers

Motivation and Leadership   Organizational Culture

Figure 1.6.   Triangle #3: Coworkers

Consistency of decision making in accord with the firm's value proposition is important. It allows members of the organization to see the connection between their daily responsibilities and the delivery of the firm's strategy. *Strategic leadership involves building a coherent set of organizational beliefs and practices that are aligned with the requirements of the seller's value proposition. All have responsibilities for their own behavior and for the performance of their coworkers, and strategic leaders are needed at all levels of the firm.*

This motivation and leadership role is important to consider, and it has already been established that every member of the firm has some responsibility. Recognizing that each individual's position within the firm affects the means of expressing leadership capabilities, it is suggested that strategic leadership is situational:

• *By Individual:* Recognizing that individuals respond to motivation, support, and nagging in different ways, the expression of leadership must be sensitive to the qualities of the intended followers and their relative status in the organization. Effective leaders assess their audiences and act accordingly. This aspect of situational leadership requires different patterns of interaction and motivational methods for different individuals. Some employees may be more comfortable when challenged directly; others may require a more nurturing approach. Further, individuals may respond differently in different situations. An individual who may be challenged when dealing with a familiar topic may need more gentility in less comfortable settings. The situational leader effectively diagnoses both the situation and the individual.

• *By Commitment to the Culture:* For the purposes of this book, the situational quali-ties of leadership have a different emphasis. When an organization's culture is well established and in alignment with the value proposition, leadership can be more "hands off." But empowerment is appropriate *only if* employees grasp and respond to the requisites of the delivery of the value proposition. When there is no common commitment to the firm's competitive strategy, empowerment allows individuals to undermine execution of the firm's value proposition. Leadership within this context is challenging. Attitudes and behaviors must be aggressively shaped before empow-erment can be authorized and encouraged. The appropriate leadership style for an organization depends in part on the degree to which the principles of *The Cycle of Success* are being practiced.

TRIANGLE #4: SUPERIOR PERFORMANCE

The middle triangle of *The Cycle of Success* is the result of the successful convergence of the three other triangles: that is, superior performance (see figure 1.7). The im-portant convergences involve linking the firm's competitive strategy to the design of the firm's individual operations and to motivation and leadership practices. This fourth triangle serves as the reminder that the winning organization meets buyer ex-pectations through integrated and linked internal systems and appropriately pre-pared personnel. What emerges is the simultaneous satisfaction of buyers and em-ployees, capturing the benefits of the loyalty of both. *The end result is superior financial performance, the outcome of successfully designing and delivering the firm's value proposition.*

Figure 1.7.   Triangle #4: Superior Performance

Leadership and *The Cycle of Success*

The final section of this chapter links *The Cycle of Success* to concepts of leadership. A more thorough analysis of leadership is deferred until chapter 7. But *The Cycle of Success* provides a theoretical backdrop to identify important qualities of strategic leaders. The following is intended to help the reader interpret leadership in terms of the execution of business strategy as opposed to thinking about abstract charismatic qualities of leaders.

The Cycle of Success clarifies qualities of leaders and helps to distinguish between managers and strategic leaders. Strategic leaders possess the following capabilities:

- *Visionary/Strategic:* It is frequently stated that leaders must have "vision," but in *The Cycle of Success* the idea of vision relates to the manner in which the firm seeks to secure a competitive advantage. *An abstract view of where the firm might want to be in the future is of limited use without its translation into an executable competitive strategy.*
- *Systems Thinker:* A strategic leader sees the connections between individual parts of the firm and its competitive strategy. Effective implementation of the firm's value proposition requires coordinated and integrated behaviors. Strategic leaders do not see individual practices or procedures. They see flows and connections between parts of the business as linked to the delivery of value to Type I Buyers. *Strategic leaders create organizations and operating practices that carefully coordinate the interactions and dependencies between operating areas.*
- *Effective Communicator/Motivator/Teacher:* Visions within the mind of the person in charge cannot yield superior performance unless all in the organization share and act in accord with the firm's strategy. A strategic leader articulates (1) the firm's strategy, (2) the linkages between individual operating areas, and (3) the contribution of each individual task to the delivery of the firm's competitive strategy. *The individual who sees the firm's strategy and who sees the requisites to deliver that strategy is equipped to build the hiring, compensation, and coaching systems in accord with the firm's competitive strategy.*
- *Obsessive:* Strategic leadership is not a part-time activity, nor can it be turned on and off when convenient. Strategic leaders are obsessed with the execution of the strategy in each act within the firm. *Strategic leaders are driven to align all activities in the firm with the delivery of the value proposition.*

Strategic leaders believe in their strategy. They endure short-term costs and dips in performance, making investments in the future. Tradeoffs are managed with a commitment to the strategy, and there is no period-to-period waffling based on current crises. The long-term direction prevails.

Exercise 1.4

Evaluate the leadership across your firm, some firm with which you are familiar, or Gibsonville. Use *The Cycle of Success* to shape your reply.

The qualities of strategic leadership described above are not limited to the senior-level authorities in an organization. Though the means to express strategic leadership qualities vary according to one's place in the hierarchy, the generic qualities are common. Accordingly, those at higher levels of the hierarchy must understand the importance of strategic leadership at all levels of a business and create an environment within which these qualities are nurtured and readily expressed.

Summary

This opening chapter has surveyed *The Cycle of Success*. The model shows the connections among buyer expectations, the firm's strategy, and the design of internal processes. *The Cycle of Success* is holistic. It allows the reader to see all operations, policies, practices, and behaviors in a firm in accord with the requisites of delivering the competitive strategy that serves targeted buyers. The integration of the firm's activities coincides with the notion of *managing by competitive theme.*

The model discussed over the previous pages may frustrate some readers who see it as abstract and idealistic. However, it is argued that understanding the model is the first step toward implementation. The alignment of a firm's management systems with the model may fall along a continuum and vary over time. Therefore, the reader should see the model as a process. Through education and the building of a cohesive management team, an organization may increasingly align its operations and decision making with the strategy.

The benefits to an organization are potentially very valuable. If *The Cycle of Success* is understood by the management team, a common decision-making methodology can be applied to all decisions. The end result is more effective implementation of the firm's value proposition. The firm should become a more formidable competitor. Further, as the management team operates cohesively, greater employee and buyer loyalty should emerge and reinforce one another.

In chapter 2, the buyer and seller value propositions are examined more thoroughly, and attention is given to consideration of the specific mix of elements that constitute value. In chapter 3, the concepts of strategic planning are considered more carefully, leading to chapter 4, in which the design and linkage of individual activities are developed more thoroughly. In chapter 5, the dictates of the firm's strategy are extended to human resource management practices. In chapter 6, *The Cycle of Success* is extended to management through a "measurement system." Finally, chapter 7 summarizes the discussion of strategic leadership.

Case Study: Gregory's Retirement Home Services

Exercises at the end of each chapter refer to a business in the planning stages: Gregory's Retirement Home Services.

Gregory is a recent retiree from the U.S. military, forty-five years old, with a background in facilities management and leading large numbers of modestly skilled individuals. In searching for a second career, Gregory is considering a business that provides (an as-yet-undetermined array of) personal services for the residents of a retirement community. The owners of the retirement community are considering the option to rent on-grounds office space to Gregory at a fee of $300 per month. Key to the decision is their analysis of Gregory's business plan.

The owners believe that an effective errand service will increase the value of their properties by improving the life quality of the residents. Further, upon demonstrated initial success of Gregory's Retirement Home Services, Gregory will be invited to extend the services to other communities owned by the same group of investors.

The retirement community comprises 1,750 one- and two-bedroom condominiums. The residents, aged fifty-five years or older, live fully independent and active lifestyles. The living units sell for $95,000 to $150,000, and a monthly $450 maintenance fee covers the cost of exterior maintenance, snow shoveling, grass and common area maintenance, and clubhouse activities. A supplemental fee of $150 per month is assessed to those who join the community's private golf and swim club.

There is no other errand service serving the retirement community. However, many residents are able to perform services for themselves; others enjoy the assistance of nearby family, and some services are performed by area businesses. Gregory is uncertain if a personal services business targeting this community can be profitable; nor is he clear about its shape, costs, and operations.

Gregory's Retirement Home Services: Exercise 1

1. Prepare a list of services that Gregory's firm might offer residents (may be revised later)
2. Develop a five-year spreadsheet in which you estimate the gross revenues to be earned based on the following assumptions you make (and show):
   - the services offered and the prices
   - the number of buyers of each service
   - the frequency of repeat purchase (costs are estimated at the ends of chapters 3 and 4)
3. Briefly discuss each of the six corners of *The Cycle of Success*

Notes

1. James Heskett, Earl Sasser, and Leonard Schlesinger, *The Service Profit Chain* (New York: Free Press, 1997), 40.
2. Michael Porter, "What Is Strategy?" *Harvard Business Review,* Reprint #96608: 3.
3. Porter, "What Is Strategy?" 4.
4. James Collins and Jerry Porras, *Built to Last* (New York: Harper Business, 1994), 214.
5. Porter, "What Is Strategy?" 5.
6. Porter, "What Is Strategy?" 6.
7. Noel Tichy, *The Leadership Engine* (New York: Harper Row, 1997).
8. Leonard Berry, *Discovering the Soul of Service* (New York: Free Press, 1999).
9. David Maister, *True Professionalism* (New York: Free Press, 1997).

Other Reading

Adams, W. A., Cindy Adams, and Michael Bowker. *The Whole Systems Approach.* Provo, Utah: Executive Excellence Publishing, 1999.

Bennis, Warren, and Joan Goldsmith. *Learning to Lead.* Reading, Mass.: Perseus Books, 1997.

Jones, Thomas, and Earl Sasser. "Why Satisfied Customers Defect." *Harvard Business Review,* November–December 1995: 88–102.

Maister, David. *Managing the Professional Service Firm.* New York: Free Press, 1993.

Scholte, Peter. *The Leadership Handbook.* New York: McGraw-Hill, 1998.

CHAPTER 2

The Value Equation
and the Nature of Services

Whereas chapter 1 provides a broad brushstroke review of *The Cycle of Success,* chapters 2–7 look at segments of the model in detail. This section examines the buyer and seller value propositions, followed by chapter 3, which examines the seller's competitive strategy. In turn, chapters 4–7 examine the design of operations in accord with the firm's strategy, the management of human resources, management by measurement system, and strategic leadership.

This book presents a central business philosophy to "put your customers' expectations at the heart of your enterprise." While such a statement has been made many times and in many places, this book focuses on the implementation of that philosophy. The goal of becoming customer driven is developed through a holistic model of a firm that creates (1) a system to define a firm's competitive strategy, (2) a basis for theme-based management that integrates all decision making in the firm around a common competitive strategy, (3) a means to build a measurement system to monitor the execution of the strategy, (4) a guide for human resource management, (5) a personal development plan, and (6) a means to develop strategic leaders at all levels of the firm.

The successful reader of this book will gain the strategic leadership skills identified in table 2.1. The most favorable outcomes of this book are realized if several colleagues complete the reading and the exercises at the same time, perhaps with an unbiased facilitator guiding their discussions. The study of this book by a management team yields a common competitive theme to guide decision making within the team's firm. The end result should be enhanced marketplace competitiveness and a winning organization.

Table 2.1.   Abilities of Strategic Leaders

- To assess and guide the strategic planning for their firm
- To integrate operations in accord with the delivery of the firm's strategy
- To identify the requisite skills and attributes to implement the firm's strategy, establish a personal development plan, and guide the firm's human resource practices
- To translate the firm's vision and strategy into a motivating force

The Value Equation

A market is created as buyers and sellers come together, exchanging information about their preferences and objectives. Rational buyers evaluate the many choices offered by competing sellers, seeking to maximize their well-being within the constraint of their finite purchasing power. On the seller side of the market, firms vie for consumer dollars by offering a mix of product features, service, and price. The seller's goal is to create a relatively (to rivals) more favorable mix of benefits to costs for buyers and to sustain superior returns. When a mutually agreeable set of price, service, and product features is found, a voluntary transaction is completed. With this brief reminder of the nature of free markets, our starting point is the value proposition,[1] a means to analyze the competitive strategy of seller and buyer expectations.

THE VARIABLES

Figure 2.1 shows a *value proposition*. The equation is a shorthand means to summarize that which the firm offers to buyers in competition against rival sellers and that which the buyer seeks to maximize when choosing among purchase options. Buyers and sellers separately determine their value propositions, and a transaction is completed when the two mesh. Before examining the implications of the value proposition in guiding the firm, the initial step is to more closely scrutinize the generic equation.

$$\textbf{Value} = \frac{Results + Process\ Quality}{Price + Cost\ of\ Acquisition}$$

Figure 2.1. Value Proposition

RESULTS

Buyers seek the best ratio of benefits (the variables in the numerator) to costs (the variables in the denominator). Among these outcomes, buyers demand "results." Doubtlessly, an individual who takes a vehicle to a mechanic for repair expects it to be fixed. When one is engaging an attorney to write a will, a legal document is a requisite outcome. No amount of high touch service or price discount can satisfy the buyer if the results are not realized.

For complex, multifeatured goods or services, there is an array of results. For example, a car offers transportation, miles per gallon, safety features, styling, dependability, size, weight, and so on. Given limitations of acceptable production costs, time, engineering, and design capabilities, a given vehicle model cannot excel relative to rivals at each of the elements that constitute the results. Some aspects of desired result may be incompatible, for example, greater weight and safety versus more miles per gallon. One result can be enhanced only at the expense of another performance characteristic. New materials and new technologies may over time alter the mix of results that can be produced. But at any point in time, the tradeoff among the components of results must be assessed by the seller and by the buyer.

The specific mix of results offered within a seller's value proposition may be the outcome of very explicit choices. A software company may purposely choose to develop a product that is easy to use, willingly sacrificing some features or processing power. Similarly, the manufacturer of lawn and garden equipment may commit to manufacturing the industry's most durable products, accepting that the products will be heavier and require more effort by the user. Importantly, this explicit choice provides research and development (R&D), manufacturing, procurement, marketing, and other areas with a common focus. The winning organization carefully articulates its intended mix of results and guides employee actions, gaining greater consistency in operations and decisions. In contrast, the results associated with a particular good or service may emerge as an unintended consequence of many small actions of employees who lack a common commitment. For example, a men's clothing store without a clear focus may stock an admixture of merchandise amid poorly matched sales personnel, decor, and location. This firm—lacking a common focus for its decisions—is likely to be a weak competitor as rivals in the low-price market segment, contemporary style segment, or fine business clothing segment do a superior job serving their target group of buyers.

The winning organization carefully articulates the mix of results offered to buyers and extends a clear choice. A warehouse grocery store is different from a full-service supermarket. If buyers know what to expect and the seller meets those expectations, few buyer disappointments occur. Buyer satisfaction, loyalty, repeat purchases, and favorable word-of-mouth promotion are likely to be achieved. In contrast, a randomly delivered value proposition dilutes the competitiveness of the firm. The full-service supermarket that trims the breadth of its inventory to reduce carrying costs may significantly weaken its value proposition and dissatisfy buyers. In turn, buyer loyalty declines, there is less frequent repeat purchasing, and there is less favorable word-of-mouth promotion.[2]

PROCESS QUALITY

Process quality variables do not relate to the physical manner in which the good or service is produced; rather, process quality refers to those elements that make the purchase more convenient and pleasant. The courtesy of a retail clerk or switchboard operator may contribute to the value received by the buyer through process quality. The location of a business, the design of its facilities, its ability to operate on schedule, and the prompt return of phone calls are process quality variables. Different firms may select and weight process quality variables differently. Certainly, not all buyers are equivalently concerned about process quality. Some buyers focus primarily on price, and some seek particular results. But in industry settings in which many sellers offer comparable results, process quality can be an effective differentiator.

The balance between process quality and results is interesting to consider. The firm that overweights results at the expense of process quality may be at risk by misinterpreting the key factors valued by buyers. In professional services, buyers may be sensitive to process quality variables because of their inability to evaluate the results and because many sellers can provide equivalent results. While the results must be delivered—perhaps an accurately completed tax form—convenience, timeliness, professional appearance, respect, and courtesy may help to differentiate a firm from its rivals. Further, when a buyer approaches a transaction with anxiety, process quality variables may build buyer confidence. The general surgeon with an unusually kind and gentle bedside manner may enjoy a relatively successful medical practice while possessing technical skills equivalent to those of many other physicians. *A firm can successfully compete on the basis of relatively superior process quality, even if the results do not markedly differ from those of rivals.* In contrast, a state-of-the-art service specialist may succeed even in the absence of process quality, relying on results that few rivals can replicate.

Well-executed process quality can also affect the results. A sales clerk in an electronics store who takes the time to learn the computing needs of a potential customer may be able to recommend the most suitable machine, thereby offering to the buyer a favorable ratio of benefits to costs. For financial advisers, the linkage between results and process quality may be important. For example, the completion of a purchase or sale of a financial instrument constitutes results. But the manner in which the full-service broker interacts with buyers and learns their needs and circumstances—process quality—may determine the effectiveness of the results by properly balancing risk and reward for the particular investor. Where process quality is high, buyers may learn to trust the financial adviser, perhaps resulting in improved abilities to cross sell investment, estate, accounting, and tax-planning services.

Process quality advantages may emerge from well-designed systems. Voice mail, e-mail, cell phone, and fax help to maintain buyer–seller contacts; linked computer capabilities between seller and buyer facilitate ordering and inventory management. Internal data-sharing systems may permit a seamless flow of information among departments and provide higher levels of service. But process quality variables are often realized from the subtleties of employee behaviors while serving clients and coworkers. Courtesies, quick, and accurate exchanges of information or timely follow-ups are important process quality variables; yet process quality variables are difficult to mandate, supervise, and control. In many service settings, buyer–employee contacts occur outside a supervisor's vision. The difficulties of supervision and control make personnel selection, training, and reward systems increasingly vital in the execution of the seller's value proposition.

PRICE

The price variable is straightforward. It is the price of the good or service, including discounts and rebates, operating and maintenance costs, and finance charges. In some settings, the price variable holds predominant weight in the value proposition. In markets or market segments where buyers cannot differentiate the goods or services of rival sellers or where the product or service differences are unimportant to the buyer, competition based on price is the alternative. But a low price, unless accompanied by lower production costs, translates into a lower profit margin. Firms that cut prices to win business but do not have a corresponding cost of production advantage are weak players in their market. Such firms may survive but only with stress, unsatisfactory margins, poor morale and working conditions, low buyer loyalty, and high employee turnover rates. *Firms that rely on price discounts to lure and retain clients should seek to understand and correct their underlying competitive deficiencies.*

Some buyers may choose among sellers exclusively on the basis of price, even at the expense of process quality. This may account for the existence of warehouse stores and self-service gasoline pumps where lower process quality is accepted in exchange for lower prices. Other firms may successfully charge a higher price than rivals, provided that the buyer receives a superior benefits-to-cost ratio. The superior value is achieved through the particular mix of results or process quality offered in the seller's value proposition. *A firm may experience higher costs in differentiating its product, and these costs can be passed forward in the form of higher prices (and greater profits) if the product or service differences are sufficiently important to buyers to warrant a higher price.*

THE COST OF ACQUISITION

Often, the buyer effectively pays more than the stated price for a good or service, with the premium being the difficulties of completing the transaction. As the inverse of process quality, the cost of acquisition includes those elements that make a purchase difficult or unpleasant, including an awkward location, long lines, lengthy forms, rude or ill-trained personnel, vendor errors, and slow responses. After-purchase experiences may contribute to the cost of acquisition through the need to return damaged or defective goods or through inferior/inhospitable service. The cost of acquisition also includes risks and uncertainties in making a purchase. A buyer may purposefully avoid a new vendor, unwilling to accept the uncertainty. This buyer behavior may inhibit the entry of new sellers, particularly in an industry in which buyer error may have serious adverse effects.

Cost of acquisition advantages may result from a superior location, well-designed operating systems that facilitate transactions, brand recognition, or unusually helpful personnel. E-commerce seeks to capture cost of acquisition advantages by allowing customers to shop from the comfort and convenience of their homes or offices rather than at a crowded mall. Convenience stores compete on the basis of low acquisition costs by providing parking in close proximity to the establishment, easy to negotiate aisles, and quick checkout. The low cost of acquisition relative to that of the supermarket makes the convenience store more attractive to some buyers for small and routine purchases. Successful franchises and brand name products reduce the cost of acquisition by providing name recognition and consistent performance, thereby reducing the risk of purchase.

Many car buyers find the purchase process inefficient and unpleasant. The decision by Saturn to operate with a "no haggle" pricing policy may reflect a strategic decision to reduce the cost of acquisition. Those buyers who dislike the usual auto showroom selling practices may prefer Saturn's value proposition, even if the vehicle's results and price are not perceived to be superior to rival automobiles. Similarly, tired travelers may opt for a nationally recognized motel chain over an independent local facility, even if such a choice carries a somewhat higher price. The higher price is acceptable to some buyers, in effect serving as an insurance policy that the room will be clean, safe, and quiet. The motel franchise that does a poor job inspecting its member units may fail to achieve consistent performance levels, and its value proposition is weakened. Similarly, the convenience store that fails to provide sufficient checkout staff at peak demand hours weakens its value proposition. Although firms do not purposefully impose costs of acquisition, they are a frequent by-product of the firm's location, personnel, behaviors and attitudes, and operating systems. Focused efforts may be needed to reduce these obstacles for the buyer, and *building a cost of acquisition advantage requires careful and thoughtful management to reduce those factors that make the transaction troublesome to buyers.*

The four variables in the value equation (results, process quality, price, and costs of acquisition) are generic headings, and each can be broken into several components. For example, results may comprise many specific variables. For example, a car's performance includes miles per gallon, acceleration, and handling characteristics. Similarly, process quality could refer to courteous sales personnel or rapid and accurate replies to questions and timely delivery of the vehicle. For sellers, it is important to articulate the *intended* and the *weighted mix of variables* in their value propositions. Two important ideas emerge:

1. Avoid the grocery list approach.
2. Weight the variables in the firm's value proposition.

Avoid the Grocery List Approach

The list of specific elements in the seller's value proposition may be lengthy, and it is vital to avoid creating a grocery list or unstructured array of items that contribute to value. Unstructured lists may confuse employees, creating a situation analogous to disorganized shopping, which frequently entails wasted time and forgotten items. In contrast, when the grocery list is organized, perhaps into sets that correspond to recipes, the shopper who understands the recipes does not need to memorize individual items. Accordingly, employees who understand their firm's value proposition are less dependent on sets of precisely defined rules and procedures.

Table 2.2 displays the differences between a disorganized grocery list—one that might emerge from an organization's brainstorming session—and a structured, recipe-based list. The example refers to a neighborhood coffeehouse and its efforts to improve customer satisfaction through managing its value proposition.

Whereas the unstructured list seems to offer good ideas, each item appears to be random and arbitrary. It is not evident why these ideas are noted and others are absent.

Table 2.2.   Means to Raise Buyer Satisfaction

Unstructured Grocery List
• Extend hours of operation
• Improve decorations
• Lower prices
• Offer different sized tables
• Offer more menu items
• Play music
• Provide magazines/paper

Recipe-Based List

Results (Selections)	Process Quality (Comfort)
• Fresh pastry	• Adjustable sound system
• Freshness	• Cleanliness
• Menu selections	• Dining room
• Nutrition content	• Restrooms
• Taste	• Soft chairs
	• Temperature control in room
	• Utensils

Price	Cost of Acquisition
• Location	• Exterior lighting
• Menu prices	• Parking
• Refills	• Safety

In contrast, the recipe-based list creates order and direction, helping to guide internal actions by displaying value-creating themes such as cleanliness, comfort, and safety. The proper labels and the effective communication of those labels direct employee behavior and stimulate creativity around value-creating themes. *The clearer the recipe-based theme, the stronger the ability to design operations that strengthen the execution of the firm's value proposition.*

Weight the Variables

In addition to the importance of identifying themes in the value proposition, the variables must be weighted by their relative importance. Because each item in the firm's value proposition cannot be the highest priority, the weights establish the relative importance of each item in the list. For example, for the hotel depicted in table 2.3, recreational facilities and luxurious rooms are the predominant elements in its value proposition. The recipe reflected in table 2.3 can be further detailed to include specific aspects of luxury, personal errand services, accommodations, furnishings, and lounge and dining facilities. *Firms with different weightings of variables in the value proposition can all be successful, but each firm must translate its particular weightings into different operating decisions. Budget allocations should be driven by the relative weightings in the value proposition, allowing the firm to allocate scarce resources according to strategy-specific priorities.*

Table 2.3.   Weighting of Variables

Variable	Percentage of Weight Given to Each Variable
Results	
Rooms/luxury	25%
• Furnishings	
Recreational facilities	30%
• Tennis courts	
• Exercise room	
Fine dining	15%
Process Quality	
Service personnel	15%
• Concierge service	
Price	10%
Cost of Acquisition	
Reservation services	5%
• Ease of use	
Total	100%

BUYER AND SELLER VALUE PROPOSITIONS

Sellers have the opportunity to choose the mix of components in the four variables that constitute the value proposition. By explicitly deciding on this mix and the relative weights, the firm communicates its intentions to potential buyers *and* to current and future employees. Within the firm, the conscious choice of the relative weights provides a means through which individual decisions are linked to the firm's competitive strategy. Not only do operational area managers gain a basis for consistency in their decision making, the seller's value proposition is also a basis for recruiting and retaining appropriate personnel. For example, some college professors prefer to work in an undergraduate teaching environment, whereas others seek employment with greater research opportunities. By clearly articulating its value proposition, a college is able to guide decision making, structure hiring and other personnel policies, and establish proper compensation systems to create an environment that facilitates the recruitment and retention of the right employees.

Gibsonville Lantern

The shift in the firm's strategy from standardized and low-priced items to customized products changes the weights in the value proposition. The relative importance of product design and customer service rises, whereas the weight assigned to price declines.

The winning firm simultaneously navigates favorable value propositions for *both* buyers and employees.[3] The resultant joint satisfaction creates mutually reinforcing cycles of (1) high morale, hard work, long-term employment, high productivity, and employee referrals and (2) loyal purchasers, positive word of mouth, and client referrals.

Exercise 2.1

A. Complete the following table for your firm, Gibsonville, or some firm with which you are familiar. In column 1, identify the specific elements that make up the value proposition. In column 2, weight these elements as implied by the firm's attitudes, decisions, and operations, noting that the sum of the weights is 100 percent. In column 3, rate the firm's performance in each area, using a scale of 1 = low to 5 = high.

Firm: _____

1	2	3
Value	**Percentage of Weight (Implied by Operations)**	**Rating**
Results		
•		
•		
Process Quality		
•		
•		
Price		
•		
Cost of Acquisition		
•		
Total	100%	

B. What changes in operation can have the greatest impact on improving value for buyers?

_____

_____

_____

Exercise 2.1 is best completed by several individuals referencing the same firm, with their separate work compared and discussed. In examining column 2, differences in replies reflect disparate beliefs about the firm's value proposition. Large differences might reveal that operating areas are driven by conflicting performance objectives. For example, a Manufacturing Department might be directed toward producing state-of-the-art products, whereas Procurement personnel might focus on low-priced inputs. Similarly, a piano maker's employees may place different weights on tonal qualities, durability, and appearance. When replies in column 2 differ markedly, it is difficult for a firm to gain consensus on decisions, to consistently improve its operations, or to allocate scarce resources among competing uses. In turn, employees are unlikely to agree on budget priorities. Any allocation is likely to breed discontent, and the leadership skills of the senior-level personnel will be questioned.

In examining column 3 in exercise 2.1, observed differences in replies reflect lack of consensus on performance ratings, and these disparities may be troublesome. Divergent performance ratings may indicate that employees hold different evaluative standards or interpret performance levels differently. In such an organization, it may be difficult to achieve standardized performance across departments or by time of day across work shifts of employees. Employees may sense unequal treatment (raises, rewards, discipline) across operating areas and feel frustrated by seemingly arbitrary decisions of management.

When differences in replies to exercise 2.1 are observed, the firm is faced with a significant challenge. It must take concerted action to clarify its competitive strategy and performance expectations throughout the organization. It is suggested in chapter 7 that no singularly successful management and leadership strategy exists. *The nature of the leadership required in a firm is a function of the commonality of view among employees of the firm's competitive strategy. When the firm's competitive strategy is clearly understood and behaviors are properly directed, a firm may enjoy a more hands-off management style. Empowerment as a management philosophy makes sense only if employees enjoy a commonly accepted competitive theme. When significant disparities exist, a more direct and controlling management style may be needed until a common view is established.*

The Nature of Services

The value equation is a useful analytic tool for any firm, and it offers particular insights for service providers. It is, however, necessary to briefly consider the nature of services and their differences from goods before applying the value equation to the service sector.

As seen in the figure below, it is suggested that the distinctions between a "good" and a "service" exist along a continuum. Rather than suggesting that there are goods and that there are services, it is argued that elements of both exist simultaneously. For a "more good-like" item, an automobile tire is denoted; for a "more service-like" item, a haircut is identified.

Good-like   *Service-like*

----

^   ^   ^

tire   Haircut

Figure 2.2. Goods versus Services Continuum

Service-like items possess the following characteristics:

• are perishable
• lack standardization
• involve buyer participation
• are intangible

For the haircut, the *perishable* aspect of services refers to the stylist's time. An hour lost today because there were no customers cannot be made up tomorrow, nor can a haircut be produced today and stored in inventory. For many service providers, this creates a set of management challenges to cope with time of day, day of week, and week-to-week or month-to-month variations in workloads and cash flow.

When performing a haircut, the service provider is engaged with the customer, accepting direction about length and style, and this represents *buyer participation* and *the inability to standardize services*. For service providers, these notions extend the transaction from results to include process quality and the cost of acquisition associated with the buyer–worker contact. The personal qualities of the service provider become an element of the buyer's experience, affecting the value delivered and received. *As such, service providers must go beyond managing the technical capabilities of their staff to managing the interactions with buyers.*

Finally, services are *intangible*. A haircut does not exist until the service has been purchased and performed. It cannot be sold from previously produced and unsold haircuts. This important aspect of services means that the buyer expresses trust and confidence that the seller can and will deliver the expected value proposition. In turn, the seller can search for ways to take advantage of this intangible quality by refining those variables that overcome a buyer's underlying reluctance to purchase that which cannot be seen. *Concerted efforts to build trust and confidence through physical appearance, marketplace reputation, and the display of professionalism by the frontline personnel may be important factors determining a firm's long-run success.*

In contrast to the haircut, the automobile tire is a tangible product. The buyer can look at the tire and touch it before making the purchase. The manufacturing plant is automated, and the particular line of tires is standardized. The tire is produced in advance of purchase and sold from inventory.

While the tire is good-like, there are elements of service associated with its sale, indicating that many items include qualities of both goods and services at the same time. The service elements include the interactions between the buyer and the retail clerk and the characteristics of the retail environment. Service may be fast or slow; the environment may be clean or dirty; the clerk may be helpful or seemingly indifferent. Further, the sales clerk may engage the buyer in conversation to determine the buyer's particular need, allowing the clerk to recommend the most appropriate tire.

As the service aspect of the tire transaction is completed successfully, the seller earns the allegiance of the buyer, raising the likelihood of the buyer repurchasing the product in the future, purchasing other automotive services from the seller (cross selling), and giving favorable word-of-mouth promotion. When the aspects of service are performed poorly, the buyer may be dissatisfied. Poor process quality or a high cost of acquisition may reduce the value received by the purchaser, weakening the competitive strength of the seller.

Gibsonville Lantern

For Gibsonville Lantern, the change in strategy to customized products involves a slide along the continuum toward greater service. Because the product does not exist at the point of purchase, the selection of features, materials, and colors involves buyer participation, and the reps must learn to conduct these new aspects of their jobs.

As firms engage differently in their businesses, their locations along the continuum are not identical. The tax preparer who focuses on the quick and inexpensive preparation of IRS forms may be more goods-like than the firm that offers comprehensive tax services. The quick tax preparer does offer some features of services, noting that the transaction must be completed quickly in a safe, clean, and secure environment. But a full-service tax preparer and consultant is well served by in-depth consultation with the buyer, explaining needs, discussing options, and planning for the future. The requisite level of trust and confidence in the ability and integrity of the full-service accounting professional is considerably greater, placing heightened emphasis on the importance of personal attributes of frontline personnel.

Frontline employees who do not fully appreciate the service aspects of their work may undermine the execution of the firm's value proposition. For example, the CPA who focuses only on doing the audit may see only the outcome (results), fail to capture process quality advantages, and fail to earn the trust of the buyer. Hence, the seller must recognize the relative importance of service-like qualities of its work in its value proposition and manage its effective execution through the proper selection, coaching, and compensation of its personnel.

A firm's position along the continuum may shift over time either by design or by default. As financial services firms adapt to the changing regulatory and competitive environment, their location on the continuum is likely to shift. Some may choose to become more goods-like, focusing primarily on executing transactions of financial instruments. Others may opt to become more service-like, engaging in the provision of advice, research, and financial planning. Different locations along the continuum alter the weighted mix of variables in the seller's value proposition and alter the firm's operating procedures and human resource practices.

Value and Performance Measures: The Firm

The final step in this section is to begin the translation of a firm's value proposition into performance measurements.[4] The measurements (1) align the value proposition

Exercise 2.2

With reference to Gibsonville Lantern, consider the goods versus service balance under the old strategy and the new strategy. Denote significant changes and discuss the implications for managing individual operations and human resources within the firm.

Old Strategy   New Strategy

_____   _____

Significant Changes

_____   _____

_____

Implications by Operating Area

Sales: _____

_____

Production: _____

_____

Finance: _____

_____

Human Resources: _____

_____

with strategy-specific performance targets for individual operating areas in the firm, (2) create an internal data set to reflect the firm's performance in those areas most important in the delivery of value to the targeted buyer, (3) provide a guide for making management decisions, (4) link the actions of each individual in the organization to key elements of performance, (5) serve as a vehicle for communicating the firm's strategy and motivate personnel by associating each task to the firm's success, and (6) provide a set of ideas that serve as a basis for strategic leadership.

Table 2.4 suggests a limited set of performance measurements for a video rental store whose value proposition heavily weights film selection and the clerks' abilities to discuss and recommend films. Importantly, the measures include goods-like qualities (film inventory) and service-like qualities (knowledge of clerks). Furthermore, the performance measures allow the firm to monitor the execution of its value proposition (days to shelf for new releases and frequency of turnover of the inventory). In turn, the firm's effectiveness in implementing its value proposition generates outcomes (frequency of repeat purchase and profits). The important messages from table 2.4 are that *the firm must monitor the execution of its value proposition and recognize that the financial performance is an outcome of the execution of the value proposition.*

Table 2.4.   Selected Performance and Outcome Measures

Selected Performance Measures	Outcome Measures
• Days to shelf for newly released film • Film knowledge of clerks • Inventory knowledge of clerks • Percentage of buyers able to get new film on initial request • Percentage of inventory not stocked by rivals • Percentage of turnover of inventory by month	• Frequency of repeat buying • Number of new customers • Percentage of clients who leave store with a film • Percentage of repeat purchasers • Profit

Gibsonville Lantern

At Gibsonville, under the new strategy, "favorable styling" may account for 30 percent of the weight in the value proposition. In turn, the performance indicator might be the number of awards won. Because the awards cannot be mandated, the associated decisions may involve the size of the design staff, spending on design tools, wages, and training.

On-time delivery—process quality—may constitute 10 percent of the weight in the value equation. The measure could be the percentage of deliveries "on time," and decisions may include the design of the production facilities.

The identification of the specific performances sought is the first step toward building a Balanced Scorecard.[5] The objective is to identify those performance criteria (column 3) that are the most important for the firm to do well, given the weighted mix of variables in the value proposition. The task in exercise 2.3 is to extend the replies from exercise 2.1 to the identification of performance measures that reflect the execution of the value proposition. Importantly, *the performance measures must be stated in ways that permit precise definition and quantification.*

In completing exercise 2.3, it must be noted that the performance measures are not directly controllable. If speed of service is important to a fast food restaurant, a manager cannot simply mandate a performance standard. Rather, appropriate operating decisions (the size of the staff, the pay and incentive systems that affect employee turnover, the equipment, and the design of the kitchen) provide the means to achieve the standard. In exercise 2.3, column 4 calls for the reader to identify decisions that may bring forth the desired performance.

The use of performance measurements to guide the implementation of the firm's value proposition is developed more thoroughly in chapter 6. For now, suffice it to suggest that (1) the intent of the table is to provide the chain linkages of actions in the firm to guide the delivery of its value proposition and (2) a management team that responds divergently to this exercise is reporting a serious problem. The team lacks consensus on how to guide and evaluate the operating performance of the firm.

Exercise 2.3

Complete the following table for your firm, Gibsonville, or some firm with which you are familiar, noting that columns 1 and 2 are identical to your reply in exercise 2.1. In column 3, identify performance measures that reflect the delivery of elements of value. In column 4, identify operating decisions that can affect the performance levels.

1	2	3	4
Value	Percentage of Weight	Measures	Decisions
Results			
•			
•			
Process Quality			
•			
•			
Price			
•			
Cost of Acquisition			
•			
Total	100%		

Explain: _____

_____

_____

Value and Performance Measures: The Individual

As performance indicators can be developed for the firm, so too can performance measures be built for each individual. As readers think about a firm's value proposition, it is reasonable to develop individual behavior and performance measures that reflect one's contribution to the delivery of the value proposition. These performance standards might be tied to technical competence and correspond to decisions on continuing education in one's specialty area. But, for other elements in the value proposition, the performance standards might include the number of hours taken to return a phone call, the percentage of days in which *The Wall Street Journal* has been read carefully, or the number of association meetings attended for a customer's industry. Additional variables may include an individual's ability to diagnose a buyer's need, to develop spontaneously a creative solution, or to act outside of a narrowly defined system. Firms can consciously build these skills through focused decisions on hiring and training and through well-designed systems that encourage employees to act on behalf of the client.[6]

Summary

This chapter creates a structure through which a firm can analyze and express the oft-stated goal of putting the customer first. The value proposition provides an organizing device that summarizes the particular weighted mix of variables offered to buyers. In turn, the value proposition provides a firm-wide basis for decision making as all operations, policies, and procedures should be designed in alignment with the execution of the firm's strategy. Finally, the development of the firm's human resources is guided as individuals are directed to acquire and hone those skills and attributes essential to implement the firm's value proposition.

In the chapters to follow, the value proposition is extended through *The Cycle of Success* to a holistic view of the firm, linking the firm's competitive strategy to all of its operations, tools, human resource capabilities, and operating policies and practices. The holistic model serves as the foundation for structuring a set of quantitative standards to guide and evaluate the firm's performance.

Gregory's Retirement Home Services: Exercise 2

1. As appropriate, revise the list of services to be offered.
2. Draft the seller's value proposition, noting the recipe-based themes and their weights.
3. Assess the value offered to buyers and propose a price strategy.
4. Define Type I Buyers and their expectations.
5. How can Gregory earn the trust of both buyers and employees?
6. Identify key internal performance indicators.

Notes

1. James Heskett, Earl Sasser, and Leonard Schlesinger, *The Service Profit Chain* (New York: Free Press, 1997), 40.
2. Leonard Berry, *Discovering the Soul of Service* (New York: Free Press, 1999), 17.
3. Berry, *Discovering the Soul of Service,* 125–57.
4. Robert Kaplan and David North, *The Balanced Scorecard* (Cambridge, Mass.: Harvard Business School Press, 1996).
5. Kaplan and North, *The Balanced Scorecard.*
6. David W. Cottle, *Client-Centered Service: How to Keep Them Coming Back for More* (New York: Wiley Press, 1990).

Other Reading

Gale, Bradley. *Managing Customer Value.* New York: Free Press, 1994.

Heskett, James, Earl Sasser, and Christopher Hart. *Service Breakthroughs.* New York: Free Press, 1990.

Reichheld, Frederick. *The Loyalty Effect.* Cambridge, Mass.: Harvard Business School Press, 1996.

Svioka, John, and Benson Shapiro. *Keeping Customers.* Cambridge, Mass.: Harvard Business School Press, 1993.

CHAPTER 3

Strategy and Value Creation

This chapter examines the nature of business strategy. It analyzes the means through which the firm seeks to capture a competitive advantage over rivals, and the themes in this chapter are

- mission statements and competitive strategy,
- strategic advantage,
- assessing competitive strategy, and
- line of business and corporate-level strategies.

Strategy and Mission

The goal of strategic planning is to position the firm to realize and sustain superior returns. The design and execution of the firm's strategy is, however, not so simple. There is no cookbook process; there is no one formula. But there is a useful framework for asking the right sets of questions. Further, whereas many think about strategic planning as a senior management function, it is argued that all in the firm must understand the strategy and everyone's decisions must be guided specifically in accord with that strategy. The firm's strategic plan must enter into its daily life and into all of its actions. Strategy must be lived at all levels of the organization!

MISSION STATEMENTS

In many organizations, strategic planning meetings/retreats begin with an examination of the firm's mission statement. A company's mission statement should express the firm's fundamental purpose and belief system, setting it apart from others in the industry. The statement should embody the business philosophy; imply the image that the firm seeks to develop; delineate the firm's primary products, markets, and services; and identify the primary needs of buyers it attempts to satisfy.[1] Unfortunately, many firms are quick to ignore their mission statements, and many mission statements suffer from the weaknesses cited in table 3.1.

Table 3.1.   Causes of Ineffective Mission Statements

- They tend to be filled with generalities and platitudes that are ambiguous
- They tend to be written in terms of the values and aspirations of the seller and not the buyer
- They tend to be written with the language of absolute rather than relative standards

These notions are examined through two fictitious mission statements. One refers to an accounting firm; the other refers to a grocery store (see table 3.2).

Table 3.2.   Mission Statements

Jones, Jones, and Jones, CPAs and Business Consultants

We are a full-service accounting firm dedicated to providing quality accounting and business consulting services to our clients. With commitments to the profession's ethical and technical standards, Jones, Jones, and Jones seeks for its owners and employees sound economic returns, collegial relationships, and a balanced lifestyle.

Greene's Grocery

Greene's is a full-service grocery store committed to serving the Northeast, focusing on offering to shoppers the widest variety of products and the freshest meats, seafood, and produce. Greene's is committed to serving our shoppers with the utmost courtesy, to attracting and retaining superior personnel, to earning profitable returns for stockholders, and to behaving as an outstanding corporate citizen within our host communities.

The Jones, Jones, and Jones (JJJ) mission statement appears to satisfy the foundation of strategic planning but may create false security. The statement is vague and fails to suggest any basis from which JJJ seeks to capture a competitive advantage over rivals. In contrast, Greene's is useful. It identifies the firm as a full-service retailer, and it focuses on outperforming rivals in critical ways. The criteria for evaluating mission statements are shown in table 3.3. Three criteria for evaluating the effectiveness of mission statements are discussed below.

Table 3.3.   Criteria to Evaluate Mission Statements

- Can the statement be unambiguously operationalized?
- Does the statement translate to a competitive strategy?
- Is the statement buyer centered?

Buyer Centered

The JJJ mission statement suggests that the seller is committed to high-quality work vended in a professional setting. The focus is on the industry's professional and ethical standards and that which the seller puts into the product and not what the buyer receives. The mix of value provided to the buyer is not defined in the mission statement, and it leaves unaddressed price, process quality, and acquisition cost concerns. The JJJ statement does not suggest to whom the firm seeks to sell. In contrast, Greene's clearly articulates its intention to offer to buyers the *widest* and *freshest* selection with the *utmost* service, effectively defining its target buyers and many of its internal operations.

Operational

The JJJ mission statement provides no operational meaning for the key term: *quality*. Because there may be several different definitions and levels of quality, the statement offers little guide for operational decision making. Does the firm want to provide "cutting-edge," highly customized services requiring the acute skills of seasoned professionals? Or is the firm engaged in routine, oft-repeated work with personal service and sensitivity to the needs of the buyer? Does *quality* refer to the technical aspects of the work, timeliness of delivery, or buyer relationships? Further, all firms claim to do quality work. But JJJ's commitment to operating at the industry's quality or technical standard is only a minimum requirement for doing business. JJJ's statement fails to provide any basis from which it can differentiate itself from its rivals. It fails to suggest the particular nature of the work that the firm wants to do, and it does not define any basis for capturing a competitive advantage over rivals.

In contrast, Greene's statement is more readily operationalized. Greene's buyers know what to do. Internally, the design of procurement practices is directed by the strategy-specific intent to offer the *freshest* products and to secure the *widest* diversity of products. Similarly, human resource systems, including hiring, rewarding, and coaching, are strategy directed to recruit and retain superior personnel and provide the *utmost* service.

Strategic

The JJJ mission statement is offered as an "absolute," as if there is quality or there is the absence of quality. This error is common as many organizations define quality in terms of the technical standards of their industry or profession. But strategy analysis is effective only if it yields *superior* and *sustained* returns, and such values are—by definition—*relative* to those of rivals. Thinking in terms of meeting the industry's professional standard fails to provide any basis for offering a relatively more attractive value proposition or earning relatively stronger financial returns. In contrast, Greene's statement is phrased in relative terms, provides a basis for differentiation from its rivals, and may yield superior financial performance.

The JJJ mission statement is generic. It could apply to almost any firm in the industry. While such a statement may have some public relations benefits, it is of little internal use. It fails to direct decision making. Yet such statements emerge from many firms for such reasons as cited in table 3.4.

An ill-defined mission statement may signal the lack of strategic leadership in an organization, reflected by an absence of competitive strategy and systems thinking. Because of the failure to complete the connection from the firm's mission to the

Table 3.4.   Causes of Ill-Defined Mission Statements

- Not being able to resolve differing opinions about the appropriate strategy, thereby settling on a bland statement for political expediency
- Not being willing or able to make hard decisions about the firm's strategy
- Not recognizing the importance of articulating a competitive strategy and linking the mission statement to ongoing behavior

strategy-specific design of its internal operations, individual employees lack direction. Decisions can be made apart from one another, yielding a mismatched set of operations and practices. Hence, internal debates about the mission are best attended to immediately. *Uncertainties about the mission that are overlooked manifest themselves later in uncoordinated decisions, low morale, and poor performance.*

Exercise 3.1

A. Consider your firm's mission statement and (1) identify the key words and (2) evaluate the clarity of the key words. Or select any firm of interest to you, display its mission statement, identify the key words, and assess the clarity of the statement.

Mission Statement	Key Words	Analysis of Clarity

B. Evaluate the mission statement using the criteria stated in table 3.3. Propose revisions to the mission statement, as appropriate.

Mission, Strategy, and the Firm's Value Proposition

A firm's mission statement must be translated into a competitive strategy. The firm needs an unambiguous statement that is directed to secure and sustain a favorable market position to earn superior returns. The "Firm" triangle in *The Cycle of Success* (see figure 3.1) is the vehicle for examining competitive strategy, its linkage with buyer expectations, and the necessities of managing internal operations in accord with the requisites of implementing the strategy.

The starting point in the analysis is the lower left corner of the triangle, competitive strategy. The goal of strategic planning is to secure a sustained advantage over rivals and to realize superior returns. A competitive advantage accrues to a firm as a result of it becoming the preferred provider for a segment of buyers. Superior financial returns are an outcome of serving buyers with a relatively more attractive value proposition, and the strength of the advantage is associated with the items listed in table 3.5.

Figure 3.1. Triangle #1: The Firm

Table 3.5.   Strength of Competitive Advantage

- The ability of rivals to replicate the value proposition
- The ability of the firm to continue to deliver the value proposition over time
- The affluence of the target group
- The importance of the particular value proposition to the target buyer
- The size of the target population

The strength of the firm's strategy depends on the importance of the firm's value proposition to the targeted buyers and the degree of difficulty rivals experience replicating the strategy. Although firms can secure an advantage over rivals in many different ways, a useful generalization is that the relative advantage is based on either a price or a product difference. While these categorizations are interesting, they are insufficient to guide the firm. More detail is needed, and the detail can emerge from an analysis of the firm's value proposition.

The value proposition (see figure 3.2) is a useful organizing device because it forces the firm to consider the particular weighted mix of variables it seeks to vend. Of course, the success of that weighted value mix depends in large part on the number and capability of rivals that offer buyers a similar value proposition. But the equation forces the firm to examine its buyers' expectations and to craft a competitive strategy around the particular mix of value-creating variables it seeks to sell. The value proposition that the firm seeks to sell should be the result of its conscious choice; it should be both *explicit* and *reasonable.*

$$\textbf{Value} = \frac{Results + Process\ Quality}{Price + Cost\ of\ Acquisition}$$

Figure 3.2. Value Proposition

EXPLICIT

While the firm has the opportunity to choose a particular value proposition, many organizations simply stumble along their way. The weighted mix of variables in the seller's value proposition is often a result of historical accident and an ill-defined culture. Some firms stumble to their value proposition because they see their goods or services too narrowly. For example, accountants do taxes and audits, and colleges sell credits and degrees. These imprecise expressions commoditize the firm's output. After all, many accounting firms and colleges perform the same technical functions. Unfortunately, where goods or services are commoditized, sellers resort to price competition to attract and retain buyers. But when no cost of production advantages are realized, price competition results in lower profit margins. Other firms stumble to a value proposition by being unwilling or unable to commit to a particular course of action or as a result of political expediency. By sidestepping debate over a firm's competitive strategy, those with differing opinions may appear to be placated. But the failure to resolve fundamental differences merely postpones difficulties, and the following problems emerge from ill-defined value propositions:

1. Limited Focus
2. Lack of Competitive Advantage
3. Lack of Direction

Limited Focus

For a barber shop, the buyer actually receives more than a haircut. There is an experience of being served, and this falls under the domain of process quality or acquisition costs. If the firm defines its service too narrowly—cutting hair—it risks failing to manage all of the opportunities to enhance value for the buyer, including decor, service provider–customer relationships, and the appearance/demeanor of the service providers. As opportunities for enhancing the value proposition are lost, the firm's competitive strength relative to rivals dwindles.

Lack of Competitive Advantage

In commoditizing its product, a firm risks being outperformed by rivals that offer a more well defined value proposition. The commoditized seller does not offer to buyers a more favorable mix of results or process quality. A lower price may be important to buyers. But if no cost of production advantage exists, the seller's financial performance is likely to be poorer than that of its more focused rivals.

Lack of Direction

The firm that is unable to translate its mission statement into operations fails to provide its employees with a common decision making focus. Individuals may make decisions with different objectives, and the sum of the individual activities within the firm is unlikely to yield an effectively delivered value proposition. For example, a multidepartment retail store may have employees who have different understandings of the firm's competitive strategy. The resultant mix of merchandise may include some items appropriate for high-income groups and other items that appeal to more modest income groups. Other manifestations of the lack of focus may include a mismatch between the merchandise and the location or decor of the store; there may be a mismatch among personnel selection, coaching and reward systems, and the merchandise mix. Inventory practices, procurement, credit policies, after-sale service, and a returns policy could also be mismatched with the merchandise mix and the expectations of the firm's Type I Buyers. In turn, shoppers are not likely to be fully satisfied by the retailer's goods or service; individual customers are unlikely to make purchases across departmental lines. Negative cycles of unhappy buyers and unhappy employees are likely to interact and threaten the profitability of the firm.

The firm that has not clarified its value proposition cannot define its Type I Buyers. Marketing initiatives cannot be focused; specific skills and knowledge of personnel cannot be leveraged; buyers are unlikely to be loyal; and financial performance may be disappointing. Importantly, a firm's employees cannot simply be directed to help recruit new business; rather, selling initiatives and rewards must be structured in accord with the firm's value proposition and Type I Buyers.

REASONABLE

Firms are free to choose their own strategic approaches to the market. While a firm may have several strategic options, it is essential to "test the reasonableness" of the alternatives before embarking on a competitive course and investing time and money. It is difficult and time consuming to reverse a poorly designed strategy. Hence, the following examinations are critical before launching a new business or a new initiative.

INTERNAL ANALYSIS

The firm must carefully study the internal resources required to implement its value proposition.[2] Three relative standards must be applied:

1. Relative to the Strategy
2. Relative to Rivals
3. Relative to Time and Place

Gibsonville Lantern

The shift in strategy to customized products appears to have occurred without the consultation of area managers. There is no evidence that John Landis was asked to identify what his area needs in order to successfully implement the new strategy. Yet it may be that the reps are inadequately trained and equipped to sell the customized products, and this weakness in the firm's resources may prevent the new strategy from being successfully implemented.

Relative to the Strategy

The firm's value proposition may require particular kinds of capabilities; hence, a firm cannot apply some abstract industrywide assessment of the needed capabilities. The strategy-specific needs must be identified, and the operative question is, *"Do we have the skills, tools, management, financial strength, and so forth to deliver our value proposition and gain a competitive advantage over rivals?"*

Gibsonville Lantern

Gibsonville Lantern may have failed to assess its internal capabilities before switching from standardized to customized products. Certainly, the essential capabilities in manufacturing shifted from assembly-line operations to a job-shop environment. Similarly, the skills and essential product knowledge of the reps changed. But there is no indication in the case that these capabilities were assessed prior to the change in strategy.

John Landis and his mid-manager colleagues are challenged to "backfill" the tools and systems. Success is, by no means, guaranteed.

For example, a local bank that aspires to be a global provider of financial services needs to examine its management staff. If no one has engaged in multinational business, engaged in foreign currency transactions, built relationships with overseas correspondent banks, or even traveled outside of national boundaries, the bank's internal capabilities may be deficient relative to its strategic aspirations. Firms that seek to compete on the basis of superior customer service—process quality—must scrutinize the quality of the tools and equipment, information systems, and personnel in terms of the requisites to deliver the superior service. The retailer of fine home furnishings may be unsuccessful—despite enjoying a fine location in an affluent community—because it lacks the financial resources to stock an inventory mix commensurate with its strategy. Importantly, *it is the firm's weakest asset relative to its strategy that limits its performance.* Embarking on a strategy for which the firm is not equipped leads to ineffective delivery of the value proposition, disappointed employees, and poor financial performance.

Relative to Rivals

The firm's strategy is intended to gain an advantage over rivals, based on price, product characteristics, or some aspect of service. Hence, the assessment of the firm's resource capabilities must be completed relative to other firms, particularly relative to those who are selling a similar value proposition. This assessment relative to rivals is difficult for many firms. It requires honest introspection to distinguish between "being good" and "being better." *Being "as good" as rivals allows the firm to be an average performer in its industry. It is only by "being better" than rivals in some way that is important to buyers that a firm secures a relative advantage.*

Gibsonville Lantern

The case indicates that Gibsonville could not compete against the larger manufacturers for shelf space at the large home centers. This weakness relative to rivals contributed to the shift in strategy. However, the case provides us with no information about Gibsonville's new, direct rivals. *It is not clear if Gibsonville has the relative capabilities to succeed as a producer of customized products.*

This assessment is difficult. There is a bias in favor of praising employees and thanking them for hard work. But the harsh reality is that superior performance results only if the firm enjoys some relative advantage over rivals. Further compounding these difficulties is that rivals seldom remain static, thereby necessitating that the firm engage in continuous improvements relative to rivals. Self-congratulations over improvements are ill-advised unless they correspond to relative gains and are not simply a matter of "keeping up."

Exercise 3.2

A. Evaluate your firm's resource base relative to the requisites of its strategy and to its rivals. Or complete the analysis for any firm with which you are familiar.

Define the competitive strategy.

_____

_____

_____

_____

B. Assess the firm's resources relative to the strategy and relative to direct rivals.

Resources	Assessment: Relative to Strategy	Assessment: Relative to Rivals
Capital Equipment		
Human Resources		
Financial Resources		
Reputation		
Marketing Channels		
Management/Leadership		
Other		

Exercise 3.2 *(continued)*

C. Given the assessments, how should the firm respond?

_____

_____

_____

_____

Gibsonville Lantern

Gibsonville is subject to changes in the nature of the market. Certainly, buyer tastes may change at any time, thereby necessitating change in the nature of the products or design. Further, the firm would be vulnerable to any significant shifts in the strategies of rivals, perhaps including their attempt to compete in the customized segment of the market. Similarly, Gibsonville's ability to work with new materials or afford new technologies must also be considered.

Relative to Time and Place

The firm must remember that it seeks a sustained advantage. The duration of any advantage may be limited because rivals, markets, and technologies are not static. Hence, the internal assessment must be made relative to the firm's ability to survive those forces that are reshaping the market. This assessment is particularly important to banks, CPA firms, brokerage houses, and other financial institutions whose regulatory environments are rapidly changing and where traditional industry boundaries are being blurred. Similar concerns exist in computing, biotech, and telecommunications industries in which technology changes at a dizzying pace. Further, all firms are subject to rivals replicating their goods or services, new products, new technologies, and mergers that alter the competitive landscape. Firms should try to anticipate significant shifts in the nature of their industry and prepare for the requisites of competing in a new environment.

EXTERNAL ANALYSIS

The second portion of the reality check is less personal and sensitive.[3] It looks outward rather than inward. The external analysis is multifaceted and complex. It involves scanning and adapting to circumstances that are outside the bounds and direct control of the firm. The analysis calls for the examination of those conditions that define the competitive landscape for the firm, and these conditions include several items:

1. The Macroeconomy
2. The Technology, Tax, Regulatory, and Social Environments
3. The Microeconomy

Gibsonville Lantern

The case indicates that the firm's sales are business-cycle sensitive, moving up and down with the strength of the economy and the level of construction and remodeling activity. Further, it can be surmised that the customization of products exposes Gibsonville to the risks of changing styles and preferences.

The Macroeconomy

Depending on the particular good or service, the market demand may be sensitive to business-cycle swings such as period-to-period changes in income, employment, or interest rates. Certainly, for many firms, the state of the economy must be extended to global considerations, including the ability of international markets to buy goods, the threat of overseas competition, and the effects of changes in exchange rates. The same logic is extended to those businesses that are sensitive to changes in interest rates. Firms engaged in economically sensitive industries must carefully monitor and forecast macroeconomic conditions and make decisions in accord with the expected direction and volatility of the economy.

The Technological, Tax, Regulatory, and Social Environments

A variety of environmental factors may create risks or opportunities. For example, the builder of exclusive beachfront vacation homes may have the skills to effectively compete, but a change in IRS allowances regarding the mortgage deduction for second homes would create an unfavorable external environment. Similarly, the video rental retailer is vulnerable to new technologies that alter the way individuals can watch movies. Because tax, regulatory, and technological forces are dynamic, the firm must try to anticipate important developments and prepare in advance. Creative firms may translate these hazards into opportunities to gain an advantage over rivals.

The Microeconomy

The assessment of the firm's microeconomic environment is important. It identifies the firm's rivals. Within an industry, firms may differ from one another by price, distribution channels, product features, technological leadership, or customer service. Despite these differences, it is frequently possible to observe groups of companies

Gibsonville Lantern

Though we know nothing of Gibsonville's direct rivals, changes in the retail environment affected Gibsonville's ability to operate under the old strategy. Large discount stores and home products stores eliminated many of Gibsonville's lumberyard and hardware outlets, contributing to the shift in strategy.

that follow a similar strategy but are different from other companies in the industry. Grouping firms within an industry by competitive strategies involves building a strategic group map.

A firm may benefit in several ways from drawing a strategic group map (see figure 3.3). First, the mapping process helps the firm identify its closest rivals, those competitors who fall within the same grid on the map. This identification is preliminary to the firm's review of its competitive strength relative to its rivals. Second, different strategic groups offer to buyers different value propositions. By recognizing these other strategic groups, a firm is better able to assess the risk of buyers migrating across the strategic group map. Finally, creative firms may look at a strategic group map of their industry and cleverly discover a new way to differentiate their goods or services.

Price

	Basic Transport	Conservative	Sporty	Conspicuous
high		Cadillac Lincoln	Jaguar	Porsche Mercedes
moderate		Taurus Cutlass		
low	Saturn Kia			

IMAGE

Figure 3.3. Strategic Group Map

Constructing a strategic group map requires identifying two qualities of an industry's competitiveness (specific elements of price, features, service, or location).[4] In figure 3.3, the automobile market serves as the example, and the industry is grouped by price and by product image. Doubtlessly, different analysts may select different variables to define strategic groups and place individual sellers in different locations. But for the purposes of this example, Cadillac is displayed as high priced and conservative, Porsche and Mercedes are high priced and conspicuous, and Saturn and Kia are low priced and basic transport.

A strategic group map helps to define the scope of a firm's competition. Differences in strategic groups may be so large that buyers are unlikely to find the goods substitutable. This would suggest that goods or services that appear to be similar may not be close competitors. A strategic group map may also help account for differences in profitability among firms within an industry; for example, one segment of the grid may be more intensely price competitive than another. Further, by examining the relative competitiveness of the different grids on a map, a firm may choose to alter its value proposition and migrate to a more attractive segment of the industry.

Line of Business and Corporate Strategies

The discussion in this chapter has focused on securing a competitive advantage for a single product or narrow line of business. The issue has been the nature of the price or product advantage that secures a favorable position for the firm. Yet a firm's strategic thinking is not limited to individual lines of business. For firms that offer an array of goods or services, the relationship among product groups involves corporate-level strategy. Three generic corporate strategies are noted in table 3.6.

Table 3.6.   Corporate-Level Strategies

- Conglomerate relationships
- Hygienic relationships
- Leveraged relationships

The identification of three generic relationships among the lines of business does not imply that they are mutually exclusive. A firm's corporate-level strategy may include aspects of more than one type of relationship. However, the categorization helps the firm (1) diagnose its intentions in offering multiple products/services, (2) identify the competitive advantages it seeks to achieve, and (3) select performance measures to monitor the execution of the corporate-level strategy.

CONGLOMERATE RELATIONSHIPS

In a conglomerate relationship, distinct lines of business operate independently. Conglomerate-like relationships may develop as a firm diversifies its mix of goods and services. A firm may intentionally redeploy assets from a stagnant and unattractive industry into an unrelated line of business that offers greater promise. Other organizations may become conglomerate-like by default either because individual lines of business (divisions) assert their "independence" or because the firm fails to manage its product or service mix and fails to capture potential synergies.

With conglomerate relationships, whether by design or default, the firm must still allocate finite resources among competing lines of business, analyzing the opportunity cost of each use of finite assets. Advisedly, the firm employs a set of weighted criteria to allocate funds among its lines of business, including growth potential, size of the capital investment needed, cash flow, risk, and the opportunity to capture a competitive advantage. Even small organizations with multiple lines of business can benefit from a formal system to allocate financial and personnel resources.

Firms may weight these resource allocation criteria differently, but all should monitor the performance of individual lines of business. Table 3.7 provides a means through which the firm may monitor its portfolio of businesses and the performance of each one.

Firms that—by default—gravitate to conglomerate relationships may lose significant profit opportunities. For example, a CPA firm may expand its range of services to

Table 3.7.   Conglomerate Relationship Performance Indicators

- Age and market share by product group
- Asset utilization by product group
- Profit by product group
- Revenue and growth rate by product group

include consulting in information technology and human resource management. These new lines of business could provide effective new streams of income, and they could reduce the firm's reliance on the increasingly competitive tax and audit business. But the diversification could be conglomerate-like (by default) if the new units are allowed to operate as separate businesses. While new income streams may be welcomed by the partners in the firm, greater benefits would accrue if the new lines of business (1) result in increased cross selling of services through one-stop shopping, (2) result in improved, integrated advice, or (3) extend the firm's "name and reputation."

HYGIENIC RELATIONSHIPS

In contrast to conglomerate relationships, hygienic relationships may exist among lines of business. Hygienic relationships may take many different forms, though all are intended to capture greater operating efficiencies. Table 3.8 identifies different forms of hygienic relationships. For example, a firm with a significant seasonal variation in its business may seek to add new products or services to smooth its cash flow, smooth the flow of work, and increase asset utilization over a year. Similarly, a firm may be able to capture economies of scale in its information system, home office administration, advertising outlays, or research by extending its product mix. Firms that have weak bargaining relationships with suppliers or buyers may seek to extend their vertical reach through backward or forward vertical integration.

Table 3.8.   Hygienic Relationships

- Align the sophistication of the work with the skill and experience composition of the staff, achieving the right mix of work and staff
- Capture scale or scope economies and improve asset utilization rates through geographic expansion or through additional products
- Smooth the month-to-month workload and cash flow
- Use vertical integration to secure more favorable access to critical inputs or more favorable access to markets

Improved hygiene can increase profitability. However, it is important to make the distinction between operating efficiencies and strategy.[5] Improved operating efficiencies are vulnerable to replication by rivals. Over the replication period, a firm may realize some temporary advantages and superior returns; yet, once hygienic initiatives are replicated by rivals, the ultimate winners are the buyers who receive improved goods or service at lower costs.

When firms are engaged in hygienic relationships, the specific gains sought need to be defined and quantified. Selected performance measures are shown in table 3.9.

Table 3.9.   Business Hygiene Benefits

- Improved asset utilization rates
- Lower input costs per unit output
- Realization of economies of scale and lower unit costs
- Smoothed month-to-month workload and cash flow

Different firms may seek to realize benefits of hygienic relationships in different ways; hence, there may be no single set of performance measures that applies in all circumstances. However, it is important for firms to identify their specific objectives in building hygienic relationships. Only with specific objectives can the firm monitor and assess its performance in implementing the corporate-level strategy. Further, because hygienic benefits do not accrue automatically, the specification of performance measures may help guide decision making and help monitor the execution of the corporate-level strategy.

LEVERAGED RELATIONSHIPS

The greatest opportunity for the firm to build profits is for it to realize synergies among the lines of business such that the total return is greater than the sum of separate parts. Synergies may improve buyer and seller value propositions in several ways. First, results may improve as more carefully integrated advice is provided. For example, a CPA who learns a client's financial circumstances may provide tax, investment, and estate planning advice more effectively than separate advisers. Second, one-stop shopping may improve process quality or lower acquisition costs. A local insurance agency that provides home, car, life, health, and business coverage offers convenience to its buyers. Additionally, an individual may feel more comfortable sharing private information with only one service provider, thereby favorably affecting the cost of acquisition. Third, core competencies may be extended over a wider variety of products, capturing advantages for the seller in multiple markets. The hotel chain that excels at providing guest services may extend those relative capabilities and capture a competitive advantage in the retirement community and nursing home industries. Finally, a brand name may be extended over a wider range of products, perhaps including the ski manufacturer who extends its name recognition advantage to clothing, other cold weather products, and winter resorts. Returns to the seller may increase as the buyer receives the benefits of confidence in a purchase based on the integrity of the brand name.

The importance of the synergy among the product lines is ultimately evaluated by the buyer, and it is important for the seller to estimate the increased benefits for the buyer through its selling several services.[6] For example, a bank may choose to extend its services to include the sale of life insurance. The advantage to buyers is one-stop shopping. But the importance of the net benefit must be weighed to assess the potential returns from the corporate strategy. How much benefit accrues to the buyer through one-stop shopping? What are the negative consequences to the buyer of breaking relations with a specialized insurance professional? Similarly, the firm that anticipates providing integrated equipment or integrated advice to a buyer must try to evaluate the net importance of that capability to the buyer. The firm may benefit from returning to the value equation, and the firm should seek to answer the questions posed in table 3.10.

Table 3.10.   Leveraged Relationships

- Does our pricing properly reflect our enhanced value to buyers?
- How are our buyers better served by our offering multiple lines of business?
- How can we measure the increase in value received by our buyers?
- How do they enhance our competitive positioning and our earning potential?
- In what ways are strengths of the firm extended over a wider range of products?
- What do we hope to accomplish from the multiple lines of business?
- What is the intended relationship between the product lines?

Responding to the questions in table 3.10 may be difficult, but the intent is to determine the impact on benefits received by the purchaser. Regardless of the measurement difficulties, estimates must be made to clarify the specific intentions of the corporate-level strategy and to prevent the firm from unwittingly overestimating its competitive advantages. The strength of a firm's corporate-level strategy depends on the importance of the enhanced benefits to the buyers as well as the likelihood that other firms will replicate the mix of goods or services.

Exercise 3.3

A. Identify the multiple lines of business conducted by your firm or a firm with which you are familiar.

Firm: _____

Lines of Business:

_____   _____   _____

_____   _____   _____

B. Describe the relationship among those lines.

_____

_____

_____

C. In what ways could the organization change to enhance the value of the multiple lines of business?

_____

_____

_____

D. Identify performance measures to help the firm monitor its success in implementing its corporate-level strategy.

Measures:

_____   _____   _____   _____   _____   _____

E. Identify specific measures of increased value to buyers as a result of your firm's multiple lines of goods or services.

Measures:

_____   _____   _____   _____   _____   _____

Summary

Strategic management refers to decision making within the firm to secure its position as a preferred provider, yielding sustained and superior returns. This chapter develops an approach to strategic analysis based on an assessment of the firm's internal and external environments and its clients' needs. The value proposition is extended to both line of business and corporate-level strategies.

Gregory's Retirement Home Services: Exercise 3

1. Write a mission statement.
2. Define and evaluate the firm's competitive strategy, noting that there are no other on-premises businesses performing personal services.
3. Prepare a plan that delineates the tools, skills, and systems needed to conduct the strategy, given the range of services you suggest for Gregory at the end of chapter 1. Be specific and estimate Gregory's costs of operations for each of years one–five.
4. If Gregory seeks to vend multiple services (interior maintenance, dog walking, errands, home repair, etc.), describe the means to best leverage the relationships among the services and identify performance measures.

Notes

1. John Pearce and Richard Robinson Jr., *Strategic Management* (Homewood, Ill.: R. D. Irwin Press, 1994), 30–56.
2. Pearce and Robinson, *Strategic Management,* 61–106.
3. Pearce and Robinson, *Strategic Management,* 172–216.
4. Michael Holt, R. Duane Ireland, and Robert Hoskisson, *Strategic Management,* 2nd edition (New York: West Publishing, 1996), 71–78.
5. Michael Porter, "What Is Strategy?" *Harvard Business Review,* Reprint #96608: 3.
6. Neil Rackham and John DeVincentis, *Rethinking the Sales Force* (New York: McGraw-Hill, 1999), 128.

Other Reading

Adams, W. A., Cindy Adams, and Michael Bowker. *The Whole Systems Approach.* Provo, Utah: Executive Excellence Publishing, 1999.
Cottle, David. *Client-Centered Service: How to Keep Them Coming Back for More.* New York: Wiley and Sons, 1990.
Maister, David. *Managing the Professional Service Firm.* New York: Free Press, 1993.

CHAPTER 4

Integrated Decisions, Operations, and Strategy

The themes in this chapter are

- aligning operations with the firm's competitive strategy,
- recognizing and managing the linkages among functional areas, and
- making decisions based on the requisites of implementing the strategy.

Strategy and Operating Areas

The overriding message of this section of the book is to *manage by competitive theme*, and the starting point is the upper triangle (the "Firm") in *The Cycle of Success* (see figure 4.1). As introduced in chapter 1, the firm's value proposition emerges from its separate activities. Any cost, service, or product feature advantage is the result, in Michael Porter's terms,[1] of doing things differently or doing different things. The notion of "activities" as the means to deliver the firm's strategy is the subject of this chapter, and the emphasis is placed on (1) the design of each functional operation in accord with the strategy and (2) the appropriate linkages among functional area operations. This portion of the analysis is developed through the eyes of John Landis, vice president of Sales at Gibsonville Lantern.

Figure 4.1. Triangle #1: The Firm

THE SHIFT IN STRATEGY AT GIBSONVILLE

Gibsonville Lantern

Though the case provides limited information, it is reasonable to question the leadership abilities of Ted Barker Jr. It appears as if the firm launched the new strategy without having fully assessed its ability to conduct that strategy.

Based on the limited case information, it appears as if John Landis joined the firm during a transition period. Ted Barker Jr.'s decision shifted the firm's strategy from selling low-priced standardized products to selling customized items. As inferred from the many problems and challenges facing Landis, Gibsonville's functional area managers were not provided the opportunity to redesign their operations or request additional personnel and equipment as needed to implement the new strategy. John Landis and his mid-manager colleagues must adapt their areas of operation and catch up to the new strategy.

Looking more closely at the Sales Department, John Landis is responsible for a set of operational tasks, including but not limited to those cited in table 4.1. The discussion that follows examines the necessity of altering all of the activities in the Sales Department. The underlying argument is that *the design of individual operations within the firm should be strategy specific.*

Table 4.1.   Landis's Responsibilities

• Hiring	• Selecting vendors
• Preparing marketing materials	• Setting territory boundaries
• Rewarding and motivating reps	• Training

CHANGES IN OPERATIONS

Gibsonville Lantern

Tom Ryan's departure may just present a simple management challenge: find a capable replacement in a timely manner. Such ongoing tasks often keep managers in a crisis-like mode. Ryan's departure does, however, create an opportunity for the firm to examine the alignment of its hiring processes with the new strategy.

Hiring

The case indicates that Tom Ryan, a sales rep, is retiring from Gibsonville. As yet, he has not been replaced. When Landis proceeds with the hiring, he must establish a new set of criteria based on the requisites of the new strategy. Under the old strategy, hiring reps was relatively simple. The reps needed to be comfortable within the local hardware store and lumberyard market place, and it was necessary for them to maintain a predictable schedule of restocking inventory. However, the new strategy calls for an expanded skills mix. First, selling custom products through face-to-face meetings with builders, architects, and developers requires that the reps be capable of understanding and explaining the product line. Second, the new strategy requires reps to listen and to understand what buyers say about the products. Perhaps more importantly, the reps must prompt discussion of unmet and anticipated buyer needs. Finally, the new strategy requires reps who are willing to be constantly available. Because each potential order is customized, questions will arise. In a competitive marketplace, failure to respond quickly will translate into lost sales.

Vendor Selection

Under the old strategy, local hardware stores and lumberyards served as the distribution channels. With the new customized and more luxury-oriented products, the reps need to work with specialty stores as well as architects, designers, and builders. But these businesses often have very diverse clientele. The builder that specializes in "starter homes" is unlikely to be an effective outlet for Gibsonville's customized products, whereas the builder of more luxury-oriented homes is more appropriate. Under the old strategy, it may have been sufficient for the reps to place the commodity-like products in as many selling locations as possible. In contrast, the new strategy demands a much more careful selection and nurturing of accounts. Type I Buyers must be defined, and the reps must be taught to identify and pursue them.

Gibsonville Lantern

Landis must spend time helping the reps examine the mix of vendors in their territory and build appropriate distribution channels. Importantly, this work cannot be successfully completed without the prior definition of Type I Buyers and appropriate training, coaching, control, and reward systems.

If Gibsonville assigns these teaching duties to John Landis, he will need to spend considerably more time in the field. For this to occur, Landis will need to be relieved of some in-office tasks, suggesting the necessity of a larger support staff in the Sales Department. *The particular duties assigned to Landis, the appropriate size of his staff, and the necessary size of his operating budget are strategy specific.*

Training and Equipment

Under the old strategy, the training requirements were negligible. Each sales rep needed to understand the order process and the necessity of maintaining a schedule of meeting with the retailers. Beyond the basics of being friendly and honest, the rep's job required little technical skill. Under the new strategy, the skill and attribute requirements expand greatly as the reps must be prepared to conduct the increasingly service-like aspects of their work.

Gibsonville Lantern

Landis must prepare his staff to implement the customization strategy. The specifics of this training must respond to the requisites of the new strategy. Training should not be limited to the technical aspects of the job. The reps must also be prepared to work with builders, decorators, and architects and conduct the service aspects of the firm's value proposition.

The case references a call from Schmidt's Hardware, and the concern relates to their Gibsonville rep, Bob Johnson. Schmidt's claims that Bob Johnson does not know the merchandise. A similar piece of evidence regarding the lack of product knowledge comes from Steve Rockwell, the rep who is complaining about the deficiencies in the catalogs and his inability to answer questions. These instances may not be isolated problems caused by individuals failing to do their homework. Rather, the evidence may suggest a more systemic problem. The field force may not have been adequately prepared to conduct the new strategy.

While the case provides insufficient information to make any final determination, Landis would err by assuming that these two personnel problems are isolated and independent events. *The personnel problems may be the consequence of the shift in the strategy, and the personnel problems must be solved in accord with the requisites of executing the new strategy.* It may not be sufficient to respond only to the Johnson and Rockwell problems; *the need for a comprehensive training routine is strategy specific.*

In addition to new skills, the reps need new tools to carry out their work. Under the old strategy, merchandise was sold from retailer inventories, and the reps periodically replaced these supplies. Given the standardized products, few questions arose. However, under the new strategy of customized products, a rep's ability to make a sale depends on the rep being able to quickly answer questions about a product's features, designs, and production and delivery schedules. To meet these obligations, the reps need contemporary communications devices to be in contact with colleagues in Manufacturing, Customer Service, and Shipping. Landis needs the budget support to allow the reps to succeed. *Without adequate training and equipment, the reps will sense that the firm is not committed to their success.* Landis will find it increasingly difficult to earn the respect and cooperation of the reps, and the value proposition will not be effectively implemented.

QUOTAS, SUPERVISION, AND CONTROL

Under the old strategy, supervision and control were not a serious problem. Gibsonville expected that it would capture some proportion of an area's building and renovation activity. Hence, under the old strategy, it was simple to examine the value of

Gibsonville Lantern

Landis's supervision and control responsibilities are particularly difficult during the transition to the new strategy. In addition to the complexities of managing any change, the new strategy requires the reps to have increased product knowledge and to be quickly available and responsive to buyers. The reps must understand the new expectations, be supportive, and be held accountable.

Given the change in strategy, the problems with Bob Johnson—the Schmidt's Hardware rep who is difficult to contact—have become more serious. The discipline and coaching responsibilities are strategy specific.

Landis may well need to work with a stricter hands-on management process until the demands of the new strategy are understood and accepted by the reps. At that time, Landis can enjoy the opportunity to "empower" his staff to make decisions.

building permits within a region and assess Gibsonville's sales performance. If Gibsonville's sales for a territory fell below the projected level, an inquiry would be prompted. Under the new strategy, the Sales Department's performance may be difficult to assess for some time. Before sales can significantly improve, the reps must acquire new skills, and new vendor relationships must be developed. Landis's supervisory responsibilities are significantly expanded.

Further, the old quota system may, at least temporarily, be inappropriate. It would be useful for Gibsonville to consider rewarding the reps as they complete steps in the transition to the new strategy. Rewards of different types could be offered upon completion of training or upon the receipt of an order from a new (Type I) buyer.

TERRITORY SIZE

Under the old strategy, territories could be quite large because only periodic visits were required to replenish inventory. The new strategy demands smaller territories to allow the reps to nurture and serve individual client relationships. This concern may be a particular problem for Landis because the reps are unlikely to accept the loss of established accounts and smaller commissions. This examination of Landis's duties suggests several important ideas:

- Managing by Competitive Theme
- Everyone Affects the Implementation of the Strategy
- Solving Problems Holistically
- Mid-Level Management Dilemmas

Managing by Competitive Theme

Specific operations in the firm must be guided by the firm's competitive strategy; hence, the concept of "managing by competitive theme" is displayed through Landis's need to reformulate the Sales Department. This notion is critical. *Each operation within the firm—however small it might seem—needs to be evaluated in terms of the firm's competitive strategy.* The design of any particular activity should not be the result of benchmarking, the history of how things have been done, or some abstract logic of "good management." *The critical evaluative force is the conformity of a process or policy with the value proposition.*

This message is important for individuals at all levels of an organization. Daily tasks and responsibilities lie within a context. *An individual's ability to mesh recommendations and decisions with the firm's value proposition distinguishes strategic leaders from managers.* For example, an accounts payable manager may choose to make payments no sooner than forty-five days following receipt of an invoice. Such may appear to be good management. It protects the firm's cash position and earns some additional interest income. Further, this manager may design a very effective control system that assures that bills are not paid prior to the forty-fifth day but not after the forty-eighth day. In contrast to "doing things right," a strategic leader "does the right thing." The appropriate payment policy is one that corresponds with the execution of the firm's value proposition. If the firm needs unique inputs received on a just-in-time basis, a shorter time to payment may be appropriate despite the adverse effects on cash flow and interest in-

Exercise 4.1

A. Describe your firm's strategy or refer to some firm with which you are familiar.

Firm: _____

Strategy (same as your reply in exercises 1.2 and 3.2): _____

_____

B. For your area (or some other area) of responsibility, list in column 1 specific operations performed. In column 2, describe the design of each operation as required to implement the firm's strategy. In column 3, assess the fit (using a scale of 1 = weak and 5 = strong fit) between the actual design and the proper design. In column 4, suggest corrective actions.

1	2	3	4
Operation	**Design**	**Fit**	**Action**

Explain: _____

_____

_____

come. *"Doing the right thing" is fundamental to strategic leadership, and "the right thing" is associated with the requisites of implementing the firm's value proposition.*

Everyone Affects the Implementation of the Strategy

Everyone in an organization makes many decisions each day, and everyone's actions affect the delivery of the seller's value proposition. For example, Gibsonville reps must prioritize sales calls, and they must make personal decisions regarding their learning about design, construction, and the most favorable means to interact with their new accounts. Further, the shipping clerk makes a variety of decisions, including the durability of the packaging materials and timeliness of shipments, and each of these decisions affects the execution of the value proposition. *Strategic leadership occurs at all levels of the firm when decisions are made in the context of effectively implementing the firm's value proposition.*

The environment within which individuals make decisions—the corporate culture—often shapes their choices. For example, a hotel housekeeper may choose to quickly and courteously respond to a request for fresh towels or an extra blanket, knowing that the decision is proper because of the firm's commitment to hospitable service. For a service-focused family medical practice, the culture may lead the receptionist to take a message with precision and a sympathetic ear, as well as a pediatrician or nurse to respond promptly. In a local diner, the culture may prompt a waitress to greet patrons with a quick smile, to attentively pour beverage refills, and to quickly clear dirty dishes. *No organization can define work rules and policies that cover every decision and contingency. But those organizations that enjoy a common culture wrapped around the firm's value proposition do not need a hefty rulebook.*

Solving Problems Holistically

As Landis tries to solve his array of problems, he should not attack them piecemeal or in a crisis mode. For example, Landis must respond to Steve Rockwell's request for product information because a major sale is in jeopardy. However, a quick and crisis-oriented fix for this problem would be a response to symptoms. If Rockwell's lack of training is systemic, similar problems are bound to recur. Quickly hiring a replacement for the retiring Tom Ryan risks bringing on board a new person who is ill-equipped to implement the strategy. Also, an emergency call to Bob Johnson telling him to "get on the ball" and "get in touch with Schmidt's Hardware" may solve the immediate symptoms but leave untreated the underlying disease. If the reps have not been prepared to implement the new strategy and if the proper hiring, coaching, and reward systems have not been put in place, problems will manifest themselves again. *Landis needs to diagnose the underlying disease—the mismatch of existing processes and procedures with the new strategy—and offer a comprehensive solution.*

Mid-Level Management Dilemmas

Many of the challenges confronting Landis can be examined within the context of mid-level managing. These issues are looked at more closely in chapter 5, but for now it is important to note that the new strategy creates stress points. "Up the chain of command" from Landis's perspective, he needs more budgetary support to carry out his duties. He must convince his boss to allocate essential funds to permit the Sales Department to train and equip the reps. Also, Landis needs staff support to allow him to spend more time in the field with the reps, and he needs time to build new distribution channels.

Gibsonville Lantern

The reps may have an "independent contractor" approach to conducting their daily business. This mind-set intensifies the challenge facing Landis: to find a win–win solution with the reps. Landis must implement the new strategy to meet his responsibilities, but he cannot succeed unless the reps see the new strategy, operations, policies, and practices as being in their best interest.

Looking "across the organization," Landis needs to work collaboratively with his peers in Manufacturing, Shipping, and Customer Service. This is evidenced by his immediate need for price information from Finance, and Landis must also satisfy Elgardo Rodriguez in Manufacturing, who contends that the reps are promising delivery dates that cannot be met.

Looking "down the organization," Landis needs to find a way to earn the full cooperation of his reps. This is a difficult challenge. The independent contractor reps have seen their jobs change and their commissions shrink. They have not seen the organization respond to the change in strategy by providing them with the training and tools to succeed. Landis must understand their resistance to change and find a win–win solution.[2]

Gibsonville Lantern

Many of the challenges facing John Landis could have been prevented by strategy-specific planning. It appears as if Ted Barker Jr. failed to exercise strategic leadership responsibilities.

While Landis's circumstances are not unique, they are good reminders of the challenges and responsibilities of management. *One of the critical tasks is to create an environment within which individuals (and the firm) can succeed.* The limited information from the case suggests that Ted Barker Jr. has not properly exercised his responsibilities. Barker should not be surprised by poor performance, frequent crises, low morale, or high turnover of employees. Further, if Landis cannot create a setting in which the reps can succeed, the Sales Department will experience an array of morale and other personnel problems.

Strategy and the Connections among Operating Areas

John Landis has many problems to solve within his Sales area; however, the case also indicates that there are unresolved issues between his area and other functional areas within the firm. Landis needs data from the Finance Department, and the Sales Department needs to be properly coordinated with Manufacturing and Shipping. An internal service map can be used to identify and manage the dependencies among activities and departments.[3] Figure 4.2 displays an internal service map from the perspective of the Sales Department.

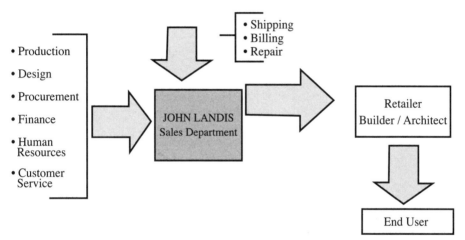

Figure 4.2. Internal Service Map: Sales Department Key Relationships

As seen in figure 4.2, the Sales Department is dependent on the successful operation of several other departments. Landis's reps cannot be successful without well-designed/styled products that are properly priced, manufactured with quality in a timely manner, and shipped without damage in accord with promised schedules. In turn, the designers may rely on the reps to gather information about buyers' assessments of the products and future needs. Other linkages exist, including Landis's (and all other departments') dependence on Human Resources to implement strategy-specific hiring and reward systems. Also, Manufacturing depends on Procurement to obtain the proper inputs as needed to meet production schedules, and the strategy-specific obligations of Procurement may depend on the conduct of Accounts Payable.

Figure 4.3 extends the internal map by another step, providing a template to summarize the needs of the unit that is the "receiver" in the interdepartmental work flow. The flow of work diagram calls for an area manager to identify the connections among operating departments, looking both forward and backward in the production process. A department may find it easy to identify its particular needs from other areas. Landis needs well-designed and customized products manufactured in a timely manner. Looking forward along the flow of work and assessing what others need from one's own department may be more difficult. *But strategy-specific performance standards and reward systems can help secure cooperation among operating areas.* For example, the Manufacturing Department at Gibsonville should not be evaluated solely on unit production costs. This would undermine its effective collaboration with Sales.

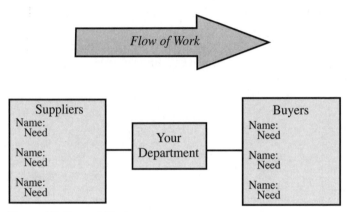

Figure 4.3. Flow of Work

Figure 4.3 emphasizes a unidirectional flow of work. Procurement meets the needs of Manufacturing, which, in turn, fills orders placed by the Sales reps. But there are important flows of work that move in the opposite direction. Manufacturing must forward to Procurement precise specifications of the inputs needed and the dates the materials are needed, and Manufacturing must receive from the reps accurate orders with achievable delivery timelines. Interdepartmental relationships involve flows of needs and responsibilities going in both directions.

One of the implications of this analysis is that *functional areas cannot be studied and guided outside of the context of the firm's overall strategy.* If specific problems are not visualized in terms of their connection with the requisites of the firm's strategy, any proposed solution is likely to be piecemeal, prove ineffective, and undermine the execution of the firm's value proposition. For example, a Telecommunications Department may recommend replacing a switchboard operating twenty-four hours per day with an automated system to save money. But this efficiency-directed recommendation may undermine the value proposition of a professional services firm that emphasizes personal attention and service. *No department operates in isolation, and no department can be allowed to make decisions outside of the requisites of delivery of the firm's value proposition.*

The proper coordination of linkages among departments requires an organizational infrastructure that facilitates the flow of information between linked areas and a reward system that supports the appropriate collaboration. *The composition of management teams and committees depends on the strategy-specific interdepartmental dependencies, and the manner in which individuals and individual operating areas are rewarded should reflect their contribution to the execution of the firm's value proposition.*

Exercise 4.2 challenges the reader to show interdepartmental connections. The flow of work and internal map diagrams suggest very important topics:

- Who Is Affected?
- Cross-Functional Teams

Exercise 4.2

A. For your area or for an operating area for a firm with which you are familiar, identify internal suppliers and internal buyers. Briefly describe what is needed from particular departmental suppliers.

1	2	3
Internal Supplier	**Needs**	**Definition of Success**

B. Briefly describe how these linkages are managed. What corrective actions would you propose?

_____

_____

_____

C. Repeat A, but identify departments that are reliant on the output of the area identified.

1	2	3
Internal Buyer	**Needs**	**Definition of Success**

WHO IS AFFECTED?

An interesting challenge for managers is to plot the path of events that are likely to follow as a result of some action taken. Figure 4.4 links the chain of events in a bank, suggesting that consequences of an action may spill widely across an organization and beyond the bounds of a manager's span of control. The analysis demands some creativity and an understanding of the linkages among events and actions within a firm, and the careful completion of such analysis may help to identify "unintended consequences."

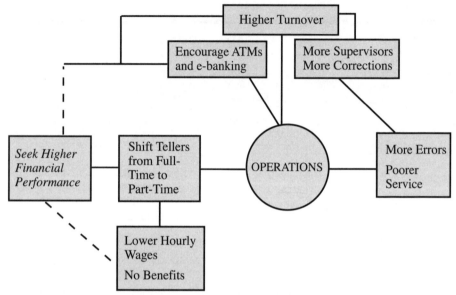

Figure 4.4. Who Is Affected?

As seen in figure 4.4, the initial decision involves a bank shifting from full-time to part-time tellers to reduce expenses and boost financial performance. Even if the bank makes the transition over time, the cause and effect events extend well beyond the initial decision. The Information Technology Department may be affected; there may be needs for more hardware and software to handle the increased reliance on electronic transactions. Human Resources may be affected through the need for more frequent hiring and training. Customer Service may be forced to respond to an increased number of errors attributable to new and inexperienced personnel.

The ultimate financial impact of the bank's decision is uncertain. However, there is the possibility that the net result of the sequenced cause and effect events will adversely affect the firm's earnings, despite the well-intended initial decision.

CROSS-FUNCTIONAL TEAMS

The bank depicted in figure 4.4 would be well served by forming a cross-functional team to investigate the option of moving to part-time tellers.[4] By bringing together individuals from the departments that are likely to be affected by a decision—a cross-functional team—the intended and unintended consequences are more likely to be properly anticipated.

The proper coordination of individual activities and departments provides another opportunity to distinguish between management and strategic leadership. *Strategic leaders see their business holistically; no operation or procedure exists in isolation. Organizational structure, teams, committees, work flows, and reward systems are designed to support the execution of the firm's value proposition.*

Assessment of the Shift in Strategy at Gibsonville

The Gibsonville Lantern case does not provide enough information to offer definitive solutions to Landis, but the following questions must be asked:

- When the firm decided to customize its products, did decision makers genuinely assess their resource base (machinery, personnel and skills, reward systems, distribution networks, etc.) to determine the firm's ability to compete successfully in the customized product market?
- Did the firm build the appropriate infrastructure to implement the new strategy?

The answers might well be no, evidenced by the incompatibility of the sales force with the new strategy, the failure to provide the reps with the essential training and tools, and the apparent mismatch between the organization's management structure and required coordination among departments. The strategy shift may have intuitive appeal because it responds to changes in the market for home building and remodeling products and because it returns the firm to its roots as a customized seller. But Ted Barker Jr. does not seem to have diagnosed the new market, assessed the requirements to successfully implement the new strategy, or allowed the organization to adapt its processes.

Corporate-Level Strategies

The prior discussion has focused on the integration of activities for a firm's line of business strategy. But, as some firms are engaged in corporate-level strategies, the nature of the integrated activities must be further examined.

CONGLOMERATE RELATIONSHIPS

In conglomerate relationships, distinct lines of business operate independently. Yet, as discussed in chapter 3, conglomerate relationships require formalized systems to allocate scarce internal resources among competing lines of business. Within a conglomerate-like setting, each line of business must be held accountable for submitting budget requests at the same time of the year. Further, each line of business must report a common set of data on its market size, market share, growth potential, cash flow, and competitive strength. The data are needed to assess the opportunity costs in allocating scarce resources. Only in this way can a firm assure that competing requests for assets are evaluated according to common criteria and that the opportunity cost of each budget allocation is assessed. Even modestly sized organizations need formalized capital budgeting and resource allocations procedures.

HYGIENIC RELATIONSHIPS

Hygienic relationships are driven by the search for improved efficiencies. The firm may seek to seasonally smooth its workload or cash flow, more fully utilize its fixed assets, or capture scale economies in R&D, logistics, or information systems. The hygiene, however, does not accrue automatically. It must be managed. A firm may need a formal system to assure that fixed resources are properly shared and that personnel are shifted between projects to maximize their utilization. The achievement of business hygiene may place considerable demands on administrators to allocate time, space, and personnel to raise asset utilization rates. The hoped-for gains in efficiency cannot be realized unless the firm is quite precise about the nature of the hygiene sought, and specific performance measures must be defined to guide decision making and to monitor performance.

LEVERAGED RELATIONSHIPS

The search for synergies among multiple lines of business creates a host of organizational problems. Leveraged relationships are designed to improve the firm's profitability in ways that go beyond conglomerate and hygiene relationships. Conglomerate relationships may provide additional revenue streams and risk reduction through diversification, and hygienic relationships may enhance efficiencies. But leveraged relationships improve profitability through an assortment of complementarities. Importantly, the nature of the complementarities must be carefully understood and managed, lest leveraging opportunities be lost or reduced into only conglomerate or hygienic benefits.

While the leveraged benefits are potentially significant to both buyer and seller, the favorable outcomes are not realized automatically as a result of the diversification. The buyer's value proposition is not enhanced unless service providers can see the clients' needs holistically and unless the technical area information is transmitted among lines of business. Demands fall on the expertise of individual service providers and on the organization of the firm to create the appropriate infrastructure.

Summary

This chapter provides the means to examine the design of operations within the firm in accord with the delivery of the value proposition. With references to the Gibsonville Lantern case, the chapter highlights the design of specific functions within an operating area and the appropriate coordination among departments. The integration of activities is extended to consider the needs of implementing corporate-level strategies. The concept of managing by competitive theme is displayed through the linkage of operating areas to the necessity of guiding each area in accord with the dictates of the strategy.

Exercise 4.3

A. Describe (as appropriate) the corporate-level strategy and the requisite coordination among its lines of business for your firm or some firm with which you are familiar. (This is the same reply offered in exercise 3.3).

Corporate Strategy: _____

_____

_____

_____

_____   _____

B. Describe how the execution of the corporate-level strategy can be improved.

_____

_____

_____

Gregory's Retirement Home Services: Exercise 4

1. Identify a set of operations, perhaps to include marketing and promotion, order taking, billing, training, accounts receivable, and operations. Describe—in some detail—the design of each of the operations as dictated by the value proposition you drafted for Gregory in chapter 2 (revise the chapter 3 cost estimates as needed).
2. For any single operating area, identify the linkages with other areas and draft an operations plan as dictated to implement the value proposition. Draw an internal service map.
3. Prepare cost estimates by year and estimate Gregory's net revenue.

Notes

1. Michael Porter, "What Is Strategy?" *Harvard Business Review,* Reprint #96608: 2.
2. Steven Covey, *Principle-Centered Leadership* (New York: Fireside Books, 1990).
3. Benjamin Schneider and David Bowen, *Winning the Service Game* (Cambridge, Mass.: Harvard Business School Press, 1995), 197–235.
4. Glenn M. Parker, *Cross Functional Teams: Working with Allies, Enemies, and Other Strangers* (San Francisco: Jossey-Bass, 1994).

Other Reading

Bennis, Warren, Richard Mason, and Ian Mitroff. *Credibility.* San Francisco: Jossey-Bass Publishers, 1993.
Heskett, James, Earl Sasser, and Christopher Hart. *Service Breakthroughs.* New York: Free Press, 1990.

CHAPTER 5

Personal and Staff Attributes

The themes in this chapter are

- management of the human resource in accord with the strategy,
- aligning skills and attributes with the strategy, and
- building personnel development plans in accord with the strategy.

These themes involve the implementation of the firm's strategy through the management of human resources. In terms of *The Cycle of Success,* the issues reside in Triangle #2, You!

Leadership and the Human Resource

The seller's value proposition is delivered through people, and this chapter builds on the notion that the requisite skill and attribute set extends beyond professional degrees, licenses, or technical training. All of the personal qualities that affect the execution of the seller's value proposition are critical in building favorable cycles of employee and client loyalty.[1] As noted in table 5.1, strategic leaders recognize the importance of their personnel and build strategy-specific human resource practices.

Table 5.1.   Selected Strategic Leadership Qualities

- Strategic leaders are effective teachers, and they help their coworkers understand (1) the firm's value proposition, (2) the relationship of each task to the delivery of the value proposition, and (3) the dependencies among functional areas of the firm
- Strategic leaders recognize that they cannot control the actions of each employee and focus instead on designing the appropriate systems and culture
- Strategic leadership falls on all members of the organization, though the expression of leadership practices differs depending on one's position in the firm

It is tempting to attribute the creation of a work environment of success to the charismatic qualities of leaders, but charisma is insufficient to overcome poorly designed practices and systems.[2] To the contrary, effectively designed practices built around the firm's competitive strategy may be sufficient to offset deficiencies in charisma. *Well-designed systems and practices configured around a consistently executed competitive strategy can yield extraordinary results as opposed to relying on extraordinary efforts to overcome poor systems or tools.*

Strategy, Skills, and Attributes

The lower left triangle in *The Cycle of Success* relates to you (see figure 5.1)! The three edges of this triangle are the firm's competitive strategy, the requisite skills and attributes you must hold to carry out your functions, and the leadership obligations that link your performance to that of your colleagues. The goal is the creation of an organizational culture that implements the firm's strategy through integrated operations.

Figure 5.1. Triangle #2: You!

The first connection to focus on is the firm's competitive strategy and the requisite skill and attribute set for each position within the firm. For example, the firm whose value proposition and competitive strategy emphasize results may place great importance on technical quality. Although no firm would express a disregard for professional quality, many firms produce routine work that demands technical competence, albeit something short of cutting-edge capability. As a result, industry standard competence may not be a source of relative advantage, though professional competence vended in particular ways may produce effective differentiation. The firm that tries to offer the relatively higher touch and speedier service should seek a certain set of human qualities in addition to industry standard competence. Hiring criteria that emphasize grade point average and academic awards may lead to the poor execution of the firm's value proposition.

The analysis of the requisite skill and attribute mix (see table 5.2) is not limited to those individuals who have direct customer contacts. Each position should be assessed in terms of what is required to conduct the firm's strategy. When an individual position includes aspects of—or is limited to—serving internal buyers, the needs of the internal buyer must be properly considered.

Gibsonville Lantern

Under the old strategy, the reps sold standardized products through local hardware stores. Under the new strategy, the reps need to develop working relationships with a different group of professionals: builders, developers, architects, and so on. The ability to sell customized products through these channels requires subtle interpersonal skills to earn trust and confidence.

Table 5.2.   Skills and Attributes

- The important assessment of the professional's personal manner, skill, and attribute mix is exercised by the buyer—and not by fellow professionals
- The requisite mix of skills and attributes depends on both the line of business strategy and the firm's corporate-level strategy
- The requisite skills and attributes extend beyond licenses and professional certifications
- The skill and attribute mix required is strategy specific, requiring the firm and employees to understand the seller's value proposition and to link the desired skill set to implementing the strategy

The second connection in Triangle #2 joins the individual's skill and attribute set to leadership and motivational obligations. The arguments are that (1) personnel policies such as hiring and compensation must be designed and implemented in accordance with the firm's strategy and (2) every person in the organization has a responsibility to help shape the attitudes and behaviors of colleagues.

Exercise 5.1 connects the skill and attribute inventory to the mix of elements in the value equation and is extended to a personal development plan. As the reader plots a personal development plan, that path should be driven by the strategic-specific needs for a position to which one aspires. Further, the strategy-specific aspects of

Exercise 5.1

Note the position to which you aspire. Position: _____

In the table below, identify in column 1 the requisite skills and attributes. In column 2, identify performance measurements. In column 3, assess your skill level as a percentage of the requisite level. In column 4, specify developmental actions.

1	2	3	4
Skill/Attribute	Measure	Assessment Rating (%)	Action Plan

skill and attribute development are readily extended to building a firm-wide human resource management process. *The important message is that the assessment of one's skill and attribute mix is strategy specific.*

Strategy, Leadership, and Motivation

The linkage between Triangles #2 (you) and #3 (your colleagues [see figure 5.2]) in *The Cycle of Success* is leadership, and this involves your obligation to understand the firm's strategy, to operate accordingly, to recognize the nature of the contributions of others, and to foster the right behaviors in colleagues. The connecting edge of the two triangles relates to a special set of strategic leadership skills that go beyond the technical ability to do one's job and to serve clients. The strategic leadership skills include several special characteristics:

1. To See Jobs in Their Larger Contexts
2. To Manage Linkages between Jobs
3. To Gather Information
4. To Engage Those Up, Down, and Across the Chain of Command
5. To Motivate

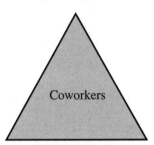

Integrated Operations

Coworkers

Motivation and Leadership   Organizational Cultur(

Figure 5.2. Triangle #3: Coworkers

TO SEE JOBS IN THEIR LARGER CONTEXTS

Gibsonville Lantern

Under the old strategy, the operation focused on long production runs to minimize production costs. Under the new strategy, Manufacturing must recognize that the focus on unit production cost is improper. Though production cannot be purposefully inefficient, the department manager must align operations with the customization and timeliness demands required to successfully implement the new strategy.

The ability to motivate and guide individuals within the organization calls for an understanding of each individual's duties and tasks in terms of delivering the firm's value proposition. All the people in the organization can understand the firm's value proposition and their role in the delivery of that proposition. The switchboard operator does not simply direct calls and take messages. In organizations where process quality and low cost of acquisition are important components of the value proposition, the switchboard operator is a vital frontline contributor. Importantly, even those individuals who do not have frontline contact with buyers make vital contributions. For example, the accurate and timely work of a data entry clerk contributes to the firm's process quality by helping customer service personnel work efficiently with buyers. *Strategic leaders help everyone in the firm to visualize the connections among their specific tasks, the firm's competitive strategy, and the joint success of the firm, the individual, and coworkers.*

Gibsonville Lantern

The essential coordination between Sales and Manufacturing is beyond the span of John Landis's management control. The linkage between those functional areas places demands on Landis's boss, within whose domain that coordination responsibility resides.

TO MANAGE LINKAGES BETWEEN JOBS

Employees at all levels of the firm are dependent on others in the organization, and these dependencies often spill across functional area boundaries. For example, an engineer who hosts a buyer meeting to review specifications of a product depends on Maintenance and Facilities to clean and properly equip an appropriate room. Even the mundane details of cleaning, scheduling, and arranging for paper, pencils, and coffee are important. But these details do not take care of themselves. Similarly, the success of an individual motel in an economy lodging franchise depends on the cost-efficient design of the facility, the selection of carpets and furniture to facilitate cleaning, and a breakfast service concept that can be staffed by a one- or two-person team. *The strategic leader is able to articulate the linkage from each task to the value proposition and effectively coordinate functional areas of operation.*

Gibsonville Lantern

The reps were in position to recognize the relative growth of discount stores and home repair stores in their territories *before* Gibsonville's sales started to slump. If that information had been communicated, Gibsonville may have been able to adapt more quickly.

TO GATHER INFORMATION

One of the important challenges for all managers is to create an environment within which subordinates are comfortable bringing forth information and, as needed, bad news. For example, an office machine repair person must feel free to report problems with the durability of a line of equipment, recognizing the adverse effects of break-downs on the execution of the firm's value proposition.

Gibsonville Lantern

John Landis is preparing a report that must outline a path to improve sales for the firm and address particular concerns of the president. Landis, reporting up the organization, is eager as a subordinate to please. But Landis must accomplish several things in the context of maintaining a good relationship with his boss. He must obtain the necessary budget support to conduct his area in accord with the new strategy and help his boss understand and manage the dependence of the Sales Department on Production, Shipping, and so on.

The reps will look over Landis's shoulders to see if their needs are well represented. Landis cannot succeed unless there is a comprehensive solution that is workable up, down, and across the organization.

TO ENGAGE THOSE UP, DOWN, AND ACROSS THE CHAIN OF COMMAND

Individuals must work within the context of their organization, which necessitates that they work with superiors, subordinates, and peers as dictated by the firm's value proposition. Each creates a separate set of problems that demands particular skills and attributes.

Working with one's boss *(up the organization)* often creates a host of problems. Doubtlessly, one's superior is responsible for creating the circumstance in which those reporting feel free to communicate good news or bad news. Also, individuals must feel free to request appropriate tools and budget support to carry out their roles in execution of the value proposition. This challenge is difficult because each operating area may think its role particularly important relative to other areas. For example, a nursing home may receive budget requests from its medical personnel seeking more nurses and equipment; food service personnel may request new and improved cooking facilities; and maintenance personnel may seek more cleaning staff. Ultimately, all requests must be evaluated in terms of their relative importance in improving the execution of the value proposition. *At all levels of the firm, strategic leaders understand their area's role in the execution of the firm's value proposition and make budget and personnel requests accordingly.*

For Landis, reporting *up the chain of command* may be a particular problem because his boss, Ted Barker Jr., seems to have failed to prepare the organization for the shift in strategy and may not understand the concept of strategy-specific needs. Without alienating Barker, Landis must play the role of teacher and help the organization through the transition to the new strategy.

The essential coordination among functional peers *(across the organization)* means that managers must handle their responsibilities within the dictates of the strategy and in compliance with the needs of dependent departments. Turf battles may occur because a firm has not clearly defined the weighted mix in its value proposition or has failed to identify the specific contributions needed from individual areas. *Turf protection must be subordinated to the requirements of the firm's value proposition, and some turf battles may be avoided by strategic leaders who convey to each area the idea of strategy-specific operations and strategy-specific needs.*

Looking down the organization, a manager cannot simply order, mandate, or threaten to secure cooperation. The mid-level management obligation includes the creation of an environment within which individuals seek to do their best work in

Gibsonville Lantern

John Landis must report to the reps as their superior. He needs their cooperation—a difficult demand as they must conduct new sets of operations in accord with the revised strategy. Landis must provide the reps with the necessary tools and training to permit them to be successful within the new strategy and to convince them of their role in the delivery of the new strategy.

Landis has a serious challenge. It appears as if the demands placed on him with regard to his staff are monumental. Landis's superiors do not seem to have created a favorable circumstance. Landis needed more lead time to prepare his staff via additional training, and he needs larger budgets for training, tools, and sales materials. Within these obstacles, Landis needs to create a win–win outcome with the reps.

Landis's boss will look over his shoulder to see if the needs of the firm are well represented and not subordinate to the self-interest of the sales reps.

Exercise 5.2

Consider the particular challenges working as a mid-level manager. Consider the particular difficulties of working up, down, and across the organization. Also, consider the strategic leader's role in facilitating the work of colleagues.

Up the organization: _____

_____

Down the organization: _____

_____

Across the organization: _____

_____

Role of Strategic Leader at Mid-Manager Levels: _____

_____

_____

delivery of the firm's value proposition. For example, John Landis must understand the nature of the reps' resistance to the new strategy, including the effects of their independent contractor status, decreases in their commissions, and the need to rebuild distribution channels. Landis is obligated to conduct the new strategy within his department. He needs to find a way to convince the reps that their best interests are served by working willingly within the new context. But Landis cannot secure their cooperation by himself. He needs the budget support to provide the necessary training and tools to demonstrate that the firm cares about the success of the reps.

TO MOTIVATE

Gibsonville Lantern

Among the many challenges facing John Landis is the need to secure the cooperation of the sales reps. Among the obstacles is the necessity that reps gather considerably more knowledge and build a new set of distribution channels. Meanwhile, the reps are experiencing declining commissions. Landis must build the right motivations and overcome the resistance of the reps.

In conducting the leadership role—connecting Triangles #2 (you) and #3 (coworkers)—the need is to gain the support of coworkers in the implementation of the firm's strategy. Because each individual may respond to incentives and stimuli differently, mid-level managers must diagnose the needs of each individual in their departments and act accordingly. Monetary and nonmonetary rewards may each be effective, but it is important to recognize that different individuals respond differently. The use of rewards and motivational techniques must be sensitive to individual circumstances. But, in addition to interpersonal qualities of situational leadership concerns, the strategic leader links individual and firm well-being through the execution of the value proposition.

Building an Organizational Culture

Building an appropriate organizational culture may be a long-term process, but a culture will emerge by design or default as a result of the myriad decisions made within a firm everyday. *The Cycle of Success* displays the linkage between the culture of the organization and the conduct of its operations. The following practices are important in building a strategy-related organizational culture aligned with the delivery of the firm's value proposition:

1. Hiring
2. Compensation and Reward
3. Coaching, Mentoring, and Nagging

4. Equipping and Training
5. Organizational Design
6. Listening
7. Managing by Theme

Gibsonville Lantern

Tom Ryan—a sales rep—is retiring, and a replacement has not yet been hired. As John Landis thinks about hiring a new sales rep, the new strategy must be translated to a new set of hiring criteria. Should Landis's hiring practices rely on old procedures, it is likely that a poor selection will be made.

HIRING

The objective is to link the firm's line of business *and* corporate-level strategies to the skills and attributes needed to succeed within each position. When filling a new or replacement position, candidates should be evaluated against a weighted set of criteria defined by the requisites of delivering the value proposition The effective organization builds a hiring grid (see exercise 5.3) in advance of preparing a job announcement and applies the grid at all stages of the recruitment, interview, and selection process to assure that the criteria are strategy specific and applied uniformly.

COMPENSATION AND REWARD

As a firm seeks to hire the right individual for each position, so too must it reward the right behaviors. The right behaviors are defined by the requisites of the delivery of the strategy, and rewards are not limited to financial payments. Great importance can be attached to a variety of nonmonetary recognitions, and these rewards must be managed as carefully as dollars and cents.

Exercise 5.4 offers a means through which an individual's work performance may be evaluated, leading to a compensation adjustment. A firm that regularly offers across-the-board fixed percentage or fixed dollar pay increases fails to reward key behaviors, thereby weakening motivation and (over time) the execution of the value proposition. Those firms that choose to operate on a merit-based system for annual increases or bonuses have an opportunity to remind their employees of their role in delivery of the firm's strategy and to reward those who are particularly successful. However, those firms that do not enjoy a clear value proposition are at risk. Any distribution of rewards that is not clearly associated with the execution of the firm's value proposition sends improper messages to their employees. Ultimately, those firms that lack a well-defined value proposition or that fail to link the value proposition to their reward systems will experience low morale, high turnover, and a weak competitive position in their industry. The purpose of exercise 5.4 is to

Exercise 5.3

For a position for which you participate in the hiring, complete the following table. In column 1, state the firm's weighted value proposition (take this information from exercise 2.1). In column 2, identify the requisite skills and attributes for the particular position. In column 3, identify the relative weights of the particular skills and attributes. In column 4, identify ways in which these skills/attributes can be assessed. Columns 5 and 6 cannot be completed: they refer to an individual applicant. But column 5 calls for the rating of the candidate's capabilities, and column 6 is the product of the weight multiplied by the rating. These products are summed and identify the highest rated candidate.

1	2	3	4	5	6
Value	Skill/Attribute	Weight	Assessment Mechanism	Rating	Product
Results					
•					
Process Quality					
•					
Price					
Cost of Acquisition					

Explain: _____

_____

weight the performance criteria in terms of the behaviors that support the firm's value proposition and to propose a compensation plan that rewards and encourages strategy-specific behaviors.

COACHING, MENTORING, AND NAGGING

Organizations need both formal and informal systems in which individuals are coached, mentored, and "nagged" about their performance as required to deliver the value proposition.[3] Different individuals at different levels of the organization have position-specific opportunities to coach, nag, and mentor. *The winning organization nurtures an environment that encourages people at all levels to review their actions in accord with the value proposition and to remind others of their strategy-specific obligations.*

Exercise 5.4

A. State the value proposition of your firm or firm of your choice (as in exercise 2.1). With reference to a position immediately below yours, describe the skills and behaviors that should be rewarded. Outline a bonus or merit pay system as it applies to a particular group of employees.

_____

_____

_____

_____

_____

_____

_____

B. Explain how the compensation system described above reinforces the delivery of the value proposition.

_____

_____

_____

EQUIPPING AND TRAINING

Gibsonville Lantern

In addition to training about the products, the reps need contemporary communications equipment. Failure to provide the equipment will weaken the execution of the value proposition, and the failure will breed among the reps low morale and a sense of organizational distrust. Recognizing the importance of immediate replies to build buyer trust and confidence, a contemporary communications system would be beneficial in support of sales and marketing.

Success must flow from hard (albeit reasonable levels of) work; _success that is dependent on extraordinary efforts is unlikely to endure._ Tools, training, and systems must be in place to implement the firm's competitive strategy; otherwise, the personnel needed to conduct the strategy will grow cynical and unproductive. The required tools are strategy specific, and the firm must provide the tools, systems, and training required to effectively implement the competitive strategy. _A firm that cannot adequately equip its personnel as required to deliver the value proposition because of budget reasons may have adopted a strategy that is inconsistent with its internal abilities._ A persistent inability to provide the means to conduct the firm's strategy results in poor financial performance and low morale as a result of the mismatch between the requisites to deliver the value proposition and the firm's assets.

ORGANIZATIONAL DESIGN

The need for effective teams in conducting multiple-level and cross-functional operations indicates the importance of proper organizational structures. The design of work flows and reporting relationships are part of the infrastructure needed for the organization to build the right systems and culture. Management must build the proper set of reporting relationships and teams to effectively implement the strategy.

Gibsonville Lantern

Under the old strategy, departments could operate independently of one another. Manufacturing could enjoy the luxury of long production runs to reduce costs and did not need to regularly communicate with Sales unless inventory levels became a problem. Under the new strategy, the interaction between these departments is much more intense. The coordination responsibilities of senior management are heightened, and it is likely that the organizational structure will have to adapt to facilitate the exchange of information. Cross-functional teams are likely to become more important within the firm.

LISTENING

At issue is building a bond between personnel and strategy so that an effective culture is built. Often, it is revealing to examine an organization's stories and heroes to determine their relationship to the value proposition. When the "heroic people and behaviors" are counter to the firm's strategy, considerable work must be done to align the culture and the strategy. Importantly, senior-level personnel must engage in an ongoing dialogue with personnel across the organization, "hear their stories," identify those who are recognized as heroes, and assess the heroic behaviors relative to the requisites of implementing the value proposition.

MANAGING BY THEME

The critical element is to manage by competitive theme. When an individual is able to articulate decisions in terms of the requisites of delivering the strategy, a consistent logic is applied. In addition to clarifying the decision, managing by competitive theme reinforces the organizational culture and builds an environment within which coworkers can be entrusted to make many decisions on their own. Once individuals understand the management theme, they will make decisions in terms of the implementation of the firm's value proposition.

Corporate-Level Strategies

The personnel development model outlined above relates to the fit of professionals' skills and traits to their firm's line of business strategy. Yet, as discussed in chapter 3, the multiple line of business organization must also manage a corporate-level strategy, and such may call for particular skills and attributes in addition to those required for the single line of business strategy.

As seen in figure 5.3, the firm's corporate-level strategy seeks gains for the buyer and for the seller. In turn, the corporate-level strategies demand particular employee skills and attributes. The nature of the skills demanded varies by the corporate-level strategy.

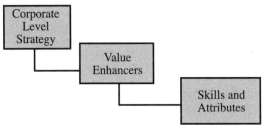

Figure 5.3. Corporate Strategies and Skills and Attributes

CONGLOMERATE RELATIONSHIPS

In a conglomerate relationship, the firm operates as a composite of several business units or divisions. Even in modestly sized firms, it is necessary for individuals to be able to assess the portfolio of businesses and allocate resources among competing units based on a common set of criteria. Further, because the mix of business units is not likely to remain static over time, individuals must recognize those units that should be eliminated and those that should be introduced. Included in the requisite skill and attribute set are the abilities to manage a diverse portfolio of businesses, to allocate resources among competing business units, and to keep the portfolio of businesses dynamic by replacing underperforming units with more promising ones.

HYGIENIC RELATIONSHIPS

In hygienic relationships, the corporate-level skills required are different. Hygienic relationships call for multiple technical skills and the ability to do different kinds of work at different times of the day or by season. These hygienic demands require an individual to accrue and maintain sufficient skills in more than one area, thereby affecting who is hired and the composition of continuing education. Further, the organization's compensation system and allocation of work assignments must foster the corporate-level strategy.

LEVERAGED RELATIONSHIPS

When the firm seeks leveraged relationships among lines of business, personnel may need a different set of skills, perhaps dependent on the particular nature of the leverage sought. For example, a technically proficient auditor may work for an accounting firm that seeks to extend its service mix to a variety of business consulting specialties. The auditor, as a frontline service provider with access to client information, must be able to recognize problems within a client's firm and have the inclination to bring the problems to the attention of other specialists within the firm. In addition to needing general business acumen to diagnose problems, the auditor must understand the firm's corporate strategy and the importance of communicating with other service providers in the firm.

Similarly, a firm that seeks to extend its core competence over a wider range of products needs several important skills. First, the firm must be sufficiently creative to identify its competence; second, that creativity must include the ability to identify areas into which the capability can be extended. For example, a firm that manufactures cameras may see itself narrowly. Or the firm may genuinely have a competence in "imaging technology." With this broader view of the firm, one must be able to identify office copying equipment and medical imaging products as appropriate options to consider in

Exercise 5.5

Describe the corporate-level strategy of your firm or a firm with which you are familiar (see exercise 3.3) and identify the particular skills and attributes you need to serve that strategy effectively. Evaluate your skills. As appropriate, suggest a personal development plan.

Corporate-Level Strategy: _____

_____

_____

_____

Requisite Skills and Attributes: _____

_____

_____

_____

Evaluation and Developmental Needs: _____

_____

_____

_____

extension of the core competence. *A leveraged corporate strategy does not accrue automatically as a result of introducing new lines of business. The specific nature of the leverage must be identified, and the staff must be capable of executing the corporate-level strategy.*

Summary

This chapter attempts to bring the firm's line of business strategy and corporate-level strategy alive through building an effective human resource model. Although the systems may appear to be somewhat contrived and rigid, the intent is to construct the thought processes that link the management of the human resource to the firm's strategy.

The procedures described in the previous pages are intended to help implement the firm's strategy. But the reader is reminded of the goal of enjoining buyers and employees into reinforcing cycles of loyalty, whereby employees enjoy satisfying buyers within the context of the firm's value proposition, work hard, refer other employees, do not leave, and generate buyer loyalty.

Gregory's Retirement Home Services: Exercise 5

Step #1: For a selected position,

1. build a hiring grid,
2. develop a compensation system, and
3. outline a staff development program.

Step #2: Use the five-year time horizon (chapter 1) to

1. estimate the size of Gregory's staff on an annual basis and estimate the wage/benefits expenses,
2. estimate the number and character of the tools needed to carry out the tasks, and
3. estimate the annual costs.

Be sure that the number and quality of the tools are strategy specific.

Notes

1. Leonard Berry, *Discovering the Soul of Service* (New York: Free Press, 1999).
2. James Collins and Jerry Porras, *Built to Last* (New York: Harper Business, 1997), 32.
3. David Maister, *Managing the Professional Service Firm* (New York: Free Press, 1993).

Other Reading

Maister, David. *True Professionalism.* New York: Free Press, 1997.
Reichheld, Frederick. *The Loyalty Effect.* Cambridge, Mass.: Harvard Business School Press, 1996.

CHAPTER 6

Leading by Measurement System

This chapter guides the development of a measurement system to implement and monitor the delivery of the firm's competitive strategy. The measurement system develops a set of variables that reflects the execution of the firm's value proposition. In turn, these strategy-specific performance measurements are linked to operating decisions that give managers opportunities to affect performance levels. The performance measures serve as a means to communicate the firm's strategy to its employees, to build a corporate culture, and to allocate finite organizational resources among competing uses as dictated by the requisites of the firm's strategy. The key themes in this chapter are

- the selection of performance indicators and
- leadership and performance measurement systems.

Managing by Performance Measures

Before a firm can develop an internal measurement system to guide decision making and monitor performance,[1] it must establish the weighted mix of variables in its value proposition. The weighted variables suggest the particular operating performances at which the firm must excel, given its strategy. The process of managing by performance measures is shown in figure 6.1.

Figure 6.1 connects the firm's value proposition and the selection of performance measures. For example, Greene's Grocery—see page 54—is focused on providing the widest selection and the freshest meats and produce. As a result, the firm can measure

---

Gibsonville Lantern

Under the old strategy, unit production costs and product durability may have been particularly important. Under the new strategy, the focus shifts to design awards won and timeliness of delivery. *Performance measures are strategy specific.*

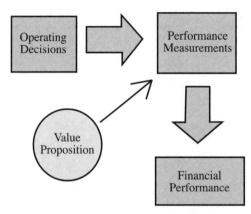

Figure 6.1. Managing by Performance
Measurements

the execution of its value proposition through the number of stock-keeping units, the time to shelve meat and produce, and the time from placement on the shelf to sale of the item. In contrast, a grocery store that competes on the basis of price should measure inventory turnover rates and the percentage of items purchased on volume discounts. *The selection of performance measures is strategy specific.*

Importantly, the performance measures are not controllable by mandate or edict. Figure 6.1 indicates that the performance measures are a result of operating decisions. For example, a firm whose value proposition emphasizes speed of service can make improvements through decisions involving training, equipment purchases, and the commitment to retain experienced employees. In turn, figure 6.1 indicates that the financial measurements of the firm's success are the lagged consequence of the firm's operating decisions and its effectiveness in the delivery of its value proposition. Several important themes arise from figure 6.1:

1. Financial Performance as a Lagging Indicator
2. Articulating the Value Proposition
3. Performance Measures, Target Values, Elasticities, and Decisions
4. Departmental and Firm-Wide Measurements
5. Model Must Be Dynamic
6. Performance Measurements and Corporate-Level Strategies

Gibsonville Lantern

The importance of winning design awards dictates decisions to staff and equip Product Development commensurate with the requirements of winning awards. The new strategy also influences the firm's financial performance goals. For example, under the old strategy, Gibsonville may have been concerned about its market share. Under the new strategy, market share will likely be smaller. Profits per retail accounts or by-products may be more significant reflectors of competitive success.

FINANCIAL PERFORMANCE AS A LAGGING INDICATOR

A firm that evaluates its performance via the analysis of financial data receives signals of its competitive performance *with a delay*.[2] Financial indicators are historical in nature; they reflect the returns to the firm over a prior period. In contrast, leading indicators of the firm's performance permit corrective actions to be put in place before financial stresses are observed. For example, a firm that manufactures products with a short technological shelf life may remain profitable for a while even as its product mix ages. But a measure of new products in the pipeline would provide the firm with an early indicator of its future profitability. Similarly, a firm that places emphasis on the durability of its product may benefit from tracking the number of breakdowns and calls for repairs, and the firm that emphasizes manufacturing precision should measure the percentage of its output that falls within its defined quality control tolerances. *Different firms will select their own set of strategy-specific measurements.*

With this perspective, the reader is reminded of the dangers associated with cost cutting to improve financial performance. While cost reductions can be appropriate, the effects of budget cuts on the delivery of the value proposition must be understood. A negative cycle of budget cuts, poor execution of the value proposition, further deterioration of financial performance, and more budget cuts is not uncommon. For example, a computer retailer that competes on the basis of customer service and advice that chooses to reduce the size of its frontline staff to cut costs may undermine the execution of its value proposition. As sales decline, it would not be uncommon to see more staff cuts. *Managerial actions must be assessed in terms of their consequences on the delivery of the seller's value proposition. Whereas senior-level executives regularly review financial reports,* all *should regularly review the performance measures that reflect the delivery of the firm's value proposition.*

ARTICULATING THE VALUE PROPOSITION

The selection of performance measurements forces the firm to define the chain links between specific aspects of its performance and its lagged financial results. In effect, the translation of the value proposition into performance measures necessitates answering the following question: *"What do we have to be (relatively) good at to succeed?"* For example, the firm whose value proposition emphasizes being first to market may concentrate on product development and innovation. Important performance measures would be the number of new product innovations per year and the length of time from product conception to sale. Related decisions would involve spending on R&D and outlays for equipment and product development personnel. Alternatively, a firm whose value proposition places significant relative weight on price should focus attention on production costs, and performance indicators should include asset utilization rates and output per man-hour. Related decisions would involve actions to reduce waste, enhance productivity, and improve the use of by-products.

Well-chosen performance measurements do significantly more than provide a monitoring and control system. They serve as a communication tool that displays to each worker that which is important to the firm's competitive success. The measures help draw the associations among each job, the delivery of the firm's strategy, and the ultimate financial performance of the enterprise. For example, the automobile manufacturer that places heavy relative weight on miles per gallon sends an important message to its design engineers. Similarly, the manufacturer of heavy-duty hoisting equipment may emphasize in its value proposition a machine's lifting capacity. In turn, the manufacturer may allocate time and money to increase the machine's lifting strength, even at the expense of its maneuverability. *Carefully selected and expressed performance measurements provide the basis for the consistent delivery of the firm's value proposition, and the measurements serve to explain decisions in the context of the firm's competitive strategy. Strategic leaders use performance measures as a teaching device, and the expression of strategy-specific "ideas" defines strategic leadership.*

As seen in figure 6.2, the fast food restaurant emphasizes speed of service in its value proposition, and speed is displayed as a performance standard. Undoubtedly, other performance measures may also be important, including cleanliness and menu selections; however, for simplicity, the diagram refers to only one performance measure. Importantly, the speed of service is a function of employee training, staff size, and equipment. Although managers cannot achieve a target level of speed by mandate, they can allocate funds among training, staff size, and equipment to affect the speed of service. In turn, the successful execution of the value proposition yields outcomes, initially in the form of buyer retention, frequency of repurchase, favorable word-of-mouth promotion, increased sales per store, and higher asset utilization rates. Ultimately, these achievements should be translated into profits and market share.

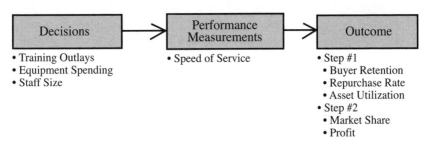

Figure 6.2. Decisions to Profit

The selection of measures of operating performance is a very important step, and it is interesting to ask several members of an organization to create a list of key performance measures. Interestingly, if the replies are widely divergent, the message is that individuals do not agree on what performance criteria are important for the success of the firm. Such would likely lead to incompatible behaviors across the firm and reflect a leadership problem.

PERFORMANCE MEASURES, TARGET VALUES, ELASTICITIES, AND DECISIONS

Once performance measures have been selected, three important ideas emerge: (1) the specification of target values for the performance measurements, (2) the association

Exercise 6.1

A. For your firm or some firm with which you are familiar, show in column 1 the weighted elements in its value proposition. (This is the same reply as that given in exercise 2.1.) In column 2, specify performance measurements. In column 3, cite operating decisions to affect the performance measurement.

1 Value	2 Performance Measurements	3 Rating
Results		
•		
•		
Process Quality		
•		
•		
Price		
•		
Cost of Acquisition		
•		
Total		

between proportionate changes in the performance measure and the associated changes in an outcome measure, and (3) the proportionate change in the performance measurement relative to an associated spending change.

Target Values

The selection of performance measurements is important but insufficient. The next step is to determine a target value for the operating measure. If speed of service is a key variable in the value proposition, one must ask, "What is the appropriate speed?" Clearly, no single answer exists for all firms. Rather, the level of performance depends on the variable's relative importance in its value proposition, its importance to Type I Buyers, and the ability of rivals to match or exceed the level.

The specification of performance target levels is crucial for a firm to determine the necessary size of its staff and the requisite tools. This is easily seen through consideration of a new start-up enterprise. In order to project future costs, there must be target performance levels, and there must be a productivity connection between those performance levels and the firm's costs.

Elasticity of Financial Outcome

The relationship shown in figure 6.3 provides a means to conceptualize the linkage between a change in a performance measure (reflecting the execution of the value proposition) and the financial consequences. For a health club, there may be an association among access to equipment, the diversity of the equipment, the size of the physical training staff, and the cleanliness of the facility. The equation does not imply that financial performance is solely a function of the percentage of change in the number of patrons who do not have to wait for equipment. Rather, the equation isolates the effect of one performance variable (waiting)—all else being equal—on profits. Hence, a similar ratio must be considered for each performance measurement. In turn, managers may use these ratios to help allocate dollars and time to affect those measures that have the greatest impact (for the incremental dollar spent) on financial performance.

Elasticity of Financial Performance $= \dfrac{Percentage\ of\ Change\ in\ Profits}{Percentage\ of\ Change\ in\ the\ Number\ of\ Patrons\ Who\ Do\ Not\ Wait\ for\ Equipment}$

Figure 6.3. Elasticity of Financial Performance

Individuals within an organization may differ in their assessment of the degree of elasticity. For example, some health club personnel may urge for more training staff, whereas others might recommend more exercise equipment; others may suggest music, improved cleanliness, or remodeling of the locker facilities. Legitimate differences of opinion may exist, and precise quantitative studies of cause–effect relationships are unlikely to provide definitive answers. But winning organizations agree on their value propositions and a common means of analysis, and they openly debate the magnitude of the relationships to arrive at the best possible decision.

Elasticity of Performance Measures

A second linkage is the connection between proportionate changes in operating outlays and proportionate changes in the performance measure. This is an important step. Managers make operating decisions (for example, spending on new equipment, salary improvements, or training) to affect performance. There is an implied linkage between the increase in resources to operate (more training) and the (expected) increase in performance. For a manufacturer, a possible connection may be between the change in spending on equipment and the resultant change in precision of its machining work, suggesting the ratio shown in figure 6.4.

Expressing the linkage in mathematical form is not intended to suggest that such a measurement is readily made. However, when the manufacturing firm makes a decision to expend more dollars on equipment, it (at least implicitly) expects payback in the form

Elasticity of Performance Measure $= \dfrac{Percentage\ of\ Change\ in\ Precision}{Percentage\ of\ Change\ in\ Equipment\ Delays}$

Figure 6.4. Elasticity of Performance Measure

of increased precision and, in turn, increased profits. The connecting degrees of sensitivity are subjectively embedded in the budget decision that allocates sums to equipment purchases, employee pay, and training. The firm is well served by expressing the cause–effect connection and estimating (albeit with uncertainty) the quantitative relationships.

Again, legitimate differences of opinion among individuals in a firm may exist. Not everyone will agree on the ratio of the proportionate changes in precision to a proportionate change in equipment spending. But winning organizations commonly accept the general linkage between decisions and performance measures, ask the questions in a common manner, and discuss the specific decisions with a common methodology.

Having established the concept of the elasticities, there are cautions:

- The measures of sensitivity are not likely to be constant over different changes in spending. The payback in product development from the first 10 percent increase in research dollars may be greater than the response to successive 10 percent increases. Similarly, the proportionate response of profits to increased spending on product development may also decline incrementally. Diminishing returns should be expected.
- The connections between performance standards and profits are not likely to be constant over time. The selection and monitoring of performance measurements allow the firm to monitor the execution of its value proposition. But it is unlikely that a firm's rivals will remain stagnant. Rivals can be expected to improve their performance over time. Hence, while it is important to monitor their own performance levels in delivering the value proposition, firms must also be conscious of their performance relative to that of rivals.
- The actual measurement of the elasticities requires an "all else being equal" assumption. For example, isolating the effect of changes in training dollars per frontline employee on accuracy of work requires that all other variables that affect accuracy are not allowed to change. In a real world situation, managers do not have the luxury of controlled experimentation; hence, the elasticity measure cannot be calculated. Still, the concept of elasticity is crucial. Without an understanding of the concept of the elasticities, managers are unable to focus on which performance measures to improve and by how much; further, without an understanding of the elasticities, managers are unable to properly allocate resources among competing uses.

DEPARTMENTAL AND FIRM-WIDE PERFORMANCE MEASURES

Gibsonville Lantern

In Gibsonville Lantern, the customization of products has significant implications for Design staff as well as for Manufacturing, Procurement, Sales, and Marketing. Doubtlessly, the effective delivery of Gibsonville's value proposition demands that each functional area operate with an internally consistent set of performance targets. A critical error would occur if Design personnel concentrated on product features while Manufacturing targeted costs of production and managed for long production runs.

The execution of the firm's value proposition demands contributions from each operating area. Recognizing that each functional area contributes to the delivery of the value proposition, there are two challenges for the firm. First, it is necessary to link the strategy to the requisite performances from each functional area. Second, each functional area must be directed by the same competitive theme. For example, a convenience store's Procurement Department must stock high-turnover merchandise, believing that speed and ease of purchase are important to buyers of frequently repurchased items. In addition, speed and ease of service require the collaboration of Human Resources to provide adequate staff to complete the transactions for purchasers, and the Real Estate Department must acquire land in high-traffic areas and secure sufficient parking. Mismatches may occur. For example, a firm whose value proposition emphasizes "error-free work" could mistakenly build a reward system that is based on piecework. An accuracy measure and speed (output per man-hour) measure may be inconsistent. *Each department must have a set of performance measures that fits with executing the firm's competitive strategy.*

The consideration of performance measurements is not limited to one or two items reflecting that which the firm must do well. For example, a retail store may consider the key elements in its value proposition to be a high-quality and contemporary product mix offered with very high touch service. Among the performance measures might be variables such as the frequency with which the store stocks new products and the skill levels of its sales personnel. In turn, operating decisions may involve procurement and inventory practices, salaries, and staff training.

In table 6.1, a full grocery store is depicted trying to deliver a particular value proposition in accord with its view of Type I Buyers. Table 6.1 indicates that the emphasis is placed on diversity of products, freshness of products, and courtesy and ease of shopping. In turn, performance measures by operating area within the firm may include the items specified in table 6.2.

Table 6.2 is not intended to be complete. Rather, the purpose is to display the link between the firm's value proposition and performance measures for each operating

Table 6.1.   Type I Buyer/Seller Value Proposition

Value Factor	Percentage of Weight Given to Each Factor
Results	40%
Selection	
Freshness	
Satisfaction of specialty orders	
Process Quality	30%
Courtesy	
Cleanliness	
Store layout	
Community relations	
Price	10%
Price of merchandise	
Cost of Acquisition	20%
Speed of checkout	
Parking access	

Table 6.2. Performance Measures by Department

Performance Measures	Target Values
Procurement	
Number of stock keeping units	_____
Shelf age of meat, seafood, and produce by product	_____
Specialty orders filled by period	_____
Housekeeping	
Time to clean up spills	_____
Time to clean up following snow storm	_____
Frequency of floor cleaning	_____
Human Resources	
Checkout time at peak load hours	_____
Marketing and Public Relations	
Dollars spent on local civic activities	_____
Operations/Design/Information Management	
Aisle width	_____
Frequency of outages	_____
Financial	
Profit margins	_____
Revenue growth	_____
Number of repeat buyers	_____

area. For each of the performance measurements, the firm must identify a target level of performance and make operating decisions to achieve those self-imposed, strategy-specific standards.

MODEL MUST BE DYNAMIC

It is important to point out that the development of a firm's set of performance measurements must have dynamic qualities because products and markets do not remain static over time. For example, a pharmaceutical firm needs to recognize the importance of introducing a stream of new products over time, and the long-term success of the firm necessitates fruitful research and development efforts. The decisions associated with the spending on research must be monitored, and the performance must be tracked, including new products in the pipeline, new patents, new product introductions, and revenue by product age.

PERFORMANCE MEASUREMENTS
AND CORPORATE-LEVEL STRATEGIES

The discussion in this chapter has, so far, been limited to the execution of the firm's line of business strategy. But this is too narrow, and the notion of managing by performance measures needs to be extended to the delivery of the firm's corporate-level strategy. The selection of measurements and the associated management decisions are related to the firm's particular corporate-level strategy.

Conglomerate Relationships

When the firm operates multiple lines of business in a conglomerate format, the separate units operate independently. But there are several measurements that should be applied to assess the strategy and guide the allocation of scarce resources among competing lines of business (see table 6.3).

Table 6.3.   Performance Measures

• Age mix of products	• Number of products
• Number of new products per year	• Profit by product
• Revenue by product	

The firm should try to monitor the number of business units as well as the revenue and costs (to include the internally allocated costs) by line of business. Because business units may be at different stages of their life cycles, the profit analysis must consider the unit's stage of life. Further, the firm engaged in aggressive conglomerate-like diversification strategy should monitor the number of new products (or services) introduced by year.

Hygienic Relationships

When the firm seeks hygienic relationships among lines of business, the objectives are improved profits through increased operating efficiencies. These measurements might include the items noted in table 6.4.

Table 6.4.   Performance Measures

- Capacity use rates for individuals, equipment, space
- Cash flow or billed hours by month
- Dollars billed by person, by rank or experience
- Percentage of work that relies on previously accumulated skills
- Percentage of work time at tasks commensurate with training and experience
- Unit production costs

Because operating efficiency is a moving target over time, the firm must establish a path of continuous improvement. Operating efficiencies are replicable by rivals; hence, the necessity is to sustain an advantage through ongoing innovation. Thus, the firm may monitor variables that reflect progress, including the introduction of new tools or processes or cost per contract or cost per account over time.

Leveraged Relationships

The leveraged relationships may present the greatest measurement difficulties. But the multiple lines of business are intended to reinforce one another by providing greater value to the buyer. Therefore, it is appropriate for the firm to monitor the data in table 6.5.

Table 6.5.   Performance Measures

- The percentage of clients who buy more than one type of good or service
- The percentage of revenue associated with multiple product sales

It is, however, important to recognize that cross selling is an outcome measure, a lagged consequence of increasing buyer value through the expansion of the range of services. This increase in value is the critical measurement used to assess the strength of the leveraged relationships. For example, the firm that seeks to offer an array of one-stop shopping services (e.g., tax, money management, financial planning, and estate planning) may seek to measure variables suggested in table 6.6.

Table 6.6.   Measures

- The number of multiple product buyers
- The value delivered to the client through improved advice and/or provision of multiple services
- The value of the client's time saved

Improvements in the number of multiple product buyers or value delivered to the buyer may occur as a consequence of the service provider's improved knowledge of an individual's (or business's) situation and needs. For example, as a CPA firm learns more about a client's firm and industry, that knowledge in a leveraged corporate-level strategy can be extended over a wider range of services. The provision of those wider services can be further enhanced as the CPA firm is able to provide theme-based, integrated advice across the client's firm.

Trying to measure the increase in value delivered to buyers is a difficult challenge.[3] There is no clear method to estimate the dollar values. In an extreme case, a tax accountant might readily measure the reduction in tax liability associated with a particular piece of advice. Such is the intent, but the dollar value of consulting advice may be more difficult to measure. But the difficulty of measurement should not discourage firms from thinking in terms of these particular measurements or from making informed estimates. The effort by the firm to qualitatively define the measurements is an important first step in shaping the firm's mind-set. In turn, operations and decisions are more likely to be made in coordination with the sought-after leverage. Even subjective assessments of the measurements may be useful, encouraging decision makers to consider the corporate-level strategy.

Summary

This chapter has provided a means through which the firm can translate its line of business and its corporate-level strategy into a set of performance targets. The measurement system is founded on the notion that financial performance is the lagged effect of the delivery of the strategy, and the measurement set provides the firm with a means to assess its delivery of value to its targeted buyers. Further, the proper selection of performance measurements serves as an expression of "theme-based" management, thus informing employees of the reasons behind management decisions.

Exercise 6.2

A. Describe the corporate-level strategy of your firm or some firm with which you are familiar.

_____

_____

_____

B. Suggest performance measurements to monitor the delivery of the corporate strategy.

_____   _____

_____   _____

C. Link operating decisions to the improvement of the metrics.

Performance Measure   **Oper**

_____   _____

_____   _____

Gregory's Retirement Home Services: Exercise 6

1. Build a Balanced Scorecard for Gregory and suggest performance targets.
2. Review your estimates of Gregory's costs (chapter 5) based on the staff size and payroll and equipment needed to meet the performance targets.

Notes

1. Robert Kaplan and David North, *The Balanced Scorecard* (Cambridge, Mass.: Harvard Business School Press, 1996).
2. Robert Kaplan and David North, "The Balanced Scorecard: Measures that Drive Performance," *Harvard Business Review*, Reprint #92105: 71–79.
3. Neil Rackham and John DeVincentis, *Rethinking the Sales Force* (New York: McGraw-Hill, 1999), 128.

Other Reading

Ferneau, Philip J. *Balancing the Corporate Scorecard: An Interactive Simulation.* Cambridge, Mass.: Harvard Business School Press, 1998.

CHAPTER 7

Leadership and *The Cycle of Success*

This chapter extends *The Cycle of Success* into a framework for analyzing leadership and building one's leadership skills. This chapter is not intended to provide a comprehensive review of the growing body of literature on leadership, nor does this chapter claim to contribute new ideas to the academic discussion of leadership. On a much more limited scale, the following pages offer a means to translate *The Cycle of Success* into leadership behaviors that the reader can apply on a daily basis.

The Cycle of Success

The Cycle of Success (see figure 7.1) seeks a convergence among the following:

- a service/product concept that fulfills buyer expectations,
- appropriately designed and linked internal operations, and
- human resource skills and an organizational culture consistent with the execution of the value proposition.

Figure 7.1. **The Cycle of Success**

As seen above, *The Cycle of Success* seeks an end result of superior performance for your firm, you, and your coworkers. The joint and simultaneous successes result from the firm's design and delivery of a value proposition that generates buyer and employee satisfaction, loyalty, repeat purchases, retained employees, and referrals of new clients and new personnel. *The Cycle of Success* provides an analytical foundation to examine and develop strategic leadership qualities across a firm.

Qualities of Strategic Leaders

LEADER AS A VISIONARY, A STRATEGIST, AND A SYSTEMS THINKER

The weighted mix of variables in the seller's value proposition defines the firm's competitive approach to the market. It formulates a guide for all of the operations, policies, and practices in the firm. The strategic leader conceptualizes the connections between each of the actions within the firm and the effective delivery of the value proposition. The concepts of "strategist" and "systems thinker" are less abstract when placed in the context of *The Cycle of Success*.

Gibsonville Lantern

Senior-level managers must receive low marks as visionaries, strategists, and systems thinkers. There is no indication in the case that the operations within the firm were analyzed in the context of executing the strategy. Those responsible for the implementation of the strategy were not given the opportunity to prepare.

Behaving within the framework of *The Cycle of Success*—to function as a strategic leader—is not beyond anyone's reach. The firm's value proposition provides a means for making consistent sets of operating decisions. Everyone's contributions to policy decisions, to affecting the decisions and behaviors of colleagues, and to building the corporate culture can be guided by the firm's value proposition. Although not everyone in an organization has equivalent influence in defining the firm's strategy, all have some ability to act on the connection among their decisions, those of their colleagues, and the firm's value proposition. Importantly, *all must see their particular tasks in the context of the firm's strategy; therefore, individuals express strategic leadership qualities by relying on the firm's value proposition as the basis for their decision making and for their guidance of colleagues.*

LEADER AS SKILLFUL, GIVEN THE STRATEGY

Each individual in an organization conducts a set of tasks, requiring some set of technical skills, personal traits, and attributes. The particular skill and attribute mix is strategy specific and not a function of general industry-wide principles. Effective leaders are obsessive and ingrain the strategy-specific principles throughout an organization. *Strategic leaders courageously make decisions based on the firm's strategy and not based on convenience or how other firms make similar decisions.*

An individual expresses a strategic leadership role by serving as an effective example by acquiring, sharpening, and demonstrating those particular qualities needed to execute the firm's value proposition. These qualities are sought at all levels of the firm, and the strategic leader helps others in the firm build appropriate skill sets.

LEADER AS COMMUNICATOR AND TEACHER

Gibsonville Lantern

Senior-level managers must, again, receive low scores. From Landis's perspective, we see the importance of gaining the support of the reps. Those senior to Landis should have provided adequate budgets to operating areas and should have redesigned the reporting systems to facilitate the interdepartmental linkages.

The delivery of the firm's value proposition is not limited to any small group of employees within the firm. While senior-level personnel and frontline employees may have more ability to display their contributions to the value proposition, everyone contributes to the delivery of the value proposition. Strategic leaders are able to help everyone in the firm see the connection between each job and the firm's competitive strategy. The teaching role occurs at all levels throughout a firm. Each individual has some ability to influence the thinking and actions of peers. *Firms must be careful to build an environment in which ideas freely arise from all stages of the hierarchy and in which all ideas are evaluated relative to the firm's value proposition.*

Gibsonville Lantern

The strategic leader sees the flow of work through an organization in terms of the requisites of delivering the firm's value proposition. In turn, the strategic leader helps all employees understand their roles in the execution of the strategy. Ted Barker Jr. does not seem to have been effective!

LEADER AS MOTIVATOR AND BUILDER OF CULTURE

The execution of the firm's value proposition happens through people who are given the correct tools, systems, and operating practices. Strategic leaders contribute to the delivery of that strategy by creating an environment in which individuals are motivated to conduct their duties in accord with the strategy. Reliance on a measurement system helps strategic leaders. Performance measures facilitate organizational communication by reminding everyone of that which is required to execute the value proposition. Regular reports to employees can update the organization's achievements, be motivational, and strengthen the organization's culture around its value proposition. *The clarity of the management theme executed through a measurement system can replace the charismatic qualities often ascribed to leaders.*

Leaders and Managers

The Cycle of Success offers an analytical construct that helps to differentiate between managers and leaders.[1] The categorization stresses that managers are prone to "do things right" but often at the expense of "doing the right things." This statement is not intended to be derogatory. It would be improper to denigrate those who seek production efficiency, to manage in accord with industry practices, and to abide by established policies and practices. However, strategic leaders go beyond standard practices. The key issue is the conformity of their operating decisions to the dictates of the seller's value proposition. A manager may, for example, carefully abide by budget allocations, whereas a strategic leader is focused on the appropriateness of budget allocations relative to the requisites of implementing the value proposition. *The important basis for evaluation of a firm's actions is their appropriateness relative to the requisites of delivering the value proposition.*

Exercise 7.1

A. For each of the descriptions listed below, denote if the phrase more appropriately defines a "manager" (M) or a "leader" (L).

1. Basis of power is "authority." _____
2. Articulates the firm's value proposition. _____
3. Works toward outcome of compliance. _____
4. Works toward outcome of commitment. _____
5. Explains decisions in terms of the firm's strategy. _____
6. Sees strengths in terms of detail, logistics, and procedures. _____
7. Diagnoses systems and linkages. _____
8. Builds collaboration around the value proposition. _____
9. Is oriented toward procedure. _____
10. Sees people as tools to complete tasks. _____
11. Sees people as long-term assets of the firm. _____
12. Focuses on meeting short-term objectives. _____
13. Thrives on ideas and connections among operations. _____
14. Defines work tasks around the firm's strategy. _____
15. Gets work done through people by assignment and mandate. _____
16. Feels need to dictate, control, and supervise all actions. _____

Exercise 7.1 *(continued)*

B. Evaluate your leadership skills and suggest actions to improve those skills.

_____

_____

_____

_____

Leadership and Situational Analysis

There is a substantial literature under the heading of "situational leadership." Much of the material is both fascinating and useful in the day-to-day expression of leadership. Keeping in mind that individuals respond to stimuli differently and have different needs,[2] readers are reminded to alter their behavior based on the characteristics of the "receiver." This aspect of situational leadership is not pursued here. Rather, the situational analysis is more limited, focusing on the degree to which the firm has adopted the principles of *The Cycle of Success.*

In chapter 1, *The Cycle of Success* was presented as a process with no ending point. *The Cycle of Success* must be understood as an idealized system, implying that no firm is likely to practice the principles in full. The favorable interactions in *The Cycle of Success* are targets. At any point in time, different firms are closer to the achievement of the favorable dynamics than others, and a firm may move closer or further away over time. *Importantly, the nature of the leadership obligation is tied to the degree to which the firm has adopted a set of guiding principles.*

Individuals—at any level of the organization—can assess the commonality of view of their immediate colleagues. The assessment vehicle may be to ask coworkers the questions in table 7.1. Upon gathering the information, a management team should examine the data suggested in table 7.1 and address the items in table 7.2.

When the replies from personnel are consistent, the leadership role is somewhat easier. With the commonality of views, leaders may engage in a more hands-off,

Table 7.1.   Assessments

* What is our firm's corporate-level strategy?
* What is the weighted value proposition for our firm?
* What performance measures should be monitored, and what are the appropriate levels of performance?

Table 7.2.   Information Sought

* To what degree do personnel have a common view of the competitive strategy?
* To what degree do they have a common set of performance objectives to assure a common delivery of the firm's value proposition?

Gibsonville Lantern

Though the case provides only limited information, we may rate Ted Barker Jr.'s leadership skills poorly. He does not seem to have understood the implications of the change in strategy for his area managers. The case does not indicate any efforts to help each operating area get ready to successfully implement the customization strategy.

empowering, consultative, and collaborative style. But when the replies are significantly disparate, the organization is more troubled, and different leadership tactics are needed.

The troubled organization must find a way to define its competitive strategy, coalesce around a value proposition, and link the value proposition to the firm's operations. *In effect, the firm's entire set of operations, decision practices, and people have to be shaped in the context of their compatibility with the value proposition. This requires a much more aggressive leadership role, but* The Cycle of Success *provides a methodology to enhance the competitive strength of the firm.*

Exercise 7.2

A. Without actually collecting data from your firm and colleagues or some firm with which you are familiar, (1) describe your expectations regarding the consistency of replies to the firm's value proposition and (2), if you expect differences, characterize the differences.

_____

_____

_____

_____

_____

_____

B. Describe how the firm's senior management can respond to the observed differences. What is your role?

_____

_____

C. How would you advise Ted Barker Jr.?

_____

_____

_____

_____

_____

Exercise 7.2 *(continued)*

D. Evaluate your strategic leadership skills. Suggest a personal development plan.

_____

_____

_____

_____

_____

_____

_____

_____

Summary

The Cycle of Success is not a leadership model based on the charismatic qualities of a select few. Quite the contrary is true. *The Cycle of Success* suggests that *strategic leadership is a matter of ideas* and that strategic leadership must occur at all levels of an organization. *The Cycle of Success* serves as a means to see the firm holistically, as a means through which all operations are analyzed, and as a means through which all decision options are assessed. By adopting the management and decision-making principles of *The Cycle of Success,* superior performance can be achieved!

Gregory's Retirement Home Services: Exercise 7

1. Prepare a brief memo to Gregory. Advise him on the responsibilities of strategic leadership.
2. Compile your answers to exercises 1–6 for Gregory's Retirement Home Services. You may change any of your replies, but you are to produce a comprehensive business and operations plan.
3. Do not see the exercise as a straightforward financial projection/business plan. Display an understanding of the holistic approach to designing and operating a business and delivering its value proposition. Make a final recommendation to Gregory!

Notes

1. Warren Bennis and Robert Townsend, *Reinventing Leadership* (New York: Harper Business, 1999).
2. Kenneth Blanchard, *Leadership and the One Minute Manager* (New York: William Morrow and Co., 1985).

Other Reading

Berry, Leonard. *Discovering the Soul of Service.* New York: Free Press, 1999.
Collins, James, and Jerry Porras. *Built to Last.* New York: Harper Business, 1997.

Postassessments

PART 1: MEMO
PART 2: SELF-ASSESSMENT

Facilitator's Guide to the Exercises

Postassessments

PART 1: MEMO

Please return to pages 5–8. Reread the memo you prepared before completing the self-study exercises.

In the space provided below, discuss the ways you would write that planning memo differently. Try to indicate how the self-study exercises influenced your thinking.

_____

_____

_____

_____

_____

_____

_____

_____

_____

_____

_____

_____

_____

_____

PART 2: SELF-ASSESSMENT

Instructions
Please complete this exercise in three steps: 1. Reply to the questions below, expressing your confidence level with each of the assignments. Use a scale of 1 to 10 (1 = low, 10 = high). Respond in column 1. 2. Refer to page 8 and reproduce your earlier replies in column 2. 3. Use the space provided at the end of the table to discuss the changes in your comfort levels as reflected in your pre- and post-self-study replies.

1	2	3
New	**Old**	**Assignment**
		You have been asked to be part of a team to develop a strategic plan for your firm.
		You have been asked to lead a team to develop a strategic plan for your firm.
		You have been asked to develop a mentoring program for new junior-level employees.
		You have been asked to develop and implement a staff evaluation system.
		You have been asked to make recommendations to correct a morale problem.
		You have been asked to define criteria for making an important hiring decision.
		You have been asked to evaluate the level of customer service extended by your firm.
		You have been asked to develop a plan to coordinate decisions among departments.
		You have been asked to define the skills and attributes to become a vice president in your firm.
		You have been asked to define the ways in which your buyers evaluate the firm's performance.
		You have been asked to develop an in-house seminar on motivation.
		You have been asked to evaluate your firm's or a client's hiring practices.
		You have been asked to evaluate the leadership in your firm or a client's firm.
		You have been asked to develop a means to assess the broad business skills of colleagues or prospective employees.
		You have been asked to develop a system to mediate differences of opinion on an important policy issue in your firm.
		You have been asked to develop a plan to distribute end-of-year raises or bonuses.

1	2	3
New	Old	Assignment
		You have been asked to define the manner in which your firm tries to gain a competitive advantage over rivals.
		You have been asked to develop an action plan to improve operating efficiencies in your firm.
		You have been asked to evaluate the organizational structure in your firm.
		You have been asked to write a personal development plan.

Revise Your Advice to John Landis and Ted Barker Jr.

(see page 13)

Facilitator's Guide to the Exercises

This guide may be used in two ways:

1. Readers may refer to the guide for additional instructions before completing the exercises and for assessing their responses. These comparisons should be made with caution. Different readers will respond to the exercises with reference to different firms, and the details of the replies are firm specific. There is no single correct answer to any exercise.
2. If this book is read by a management team or used in an undergraduate or graduate course, the guide facilitates discussion.

Chapter 1

EXERCISE 1.1 (PAGE 20)

Type I Buyers, Quality Buyer Ratio, and Action Plan

The reader is encouraged to answer in detail and extend the reply well beyond a demographic description of the firm's current buyers. Consider the purchasers' particular needs and interests that make them Type I Buyers. Estimate the firm's Quality Buyer Ratio. For the Action Plan, offer specific marketing recommendations that target Type I Buyers.

Facilitator's Note

Push participants for a detailed description of Type I Buyers. Try to gain a consensus on the definition but do not limit debate. If different opinions exist, have one participant record them for future reference. Before proceeding, ask the participants to discuss the implications of any disagreements. With regard to the Action Plan, be sure that the recommendations are specific and target Type I Buyers.

EXERCISE 1.2 (PAGE 25)

The Cycle of Success

This open-ended question cannot be completed in the space provided, and the reader should not try to comment on all aspects of the firm's operations. Avoid generalities—noting a few detailed examples is preferable to a superficial overview. Evaluate how closely the firm has adopted the principles of *The Cycle of Success*.

Facilitator's Note

The definition of the Type I Buyer offered in exercise 1.1 should be carried forward to Buyer Expectations. If disagreements persist, proceed with the majority opinion. Ask the participants to discuss the clarity of the fit among the firm's strategy, the expectations of the targeted buyers, and the design of specific operations and policies. Individuals should provide specific examples of operations and policies in their area that closely conform to the execution of the firm's strategy and do not seem to be aligned with the strategy. If the definition of Type I Buyers remains a point of disagreement, discuss the implications on the design of individual tasks.

EXERCISE 1.3 (PAGE 28)

Human Resource Management

Readers should not try to comment on all aspects of the firm's human resource management; the topic is too broad. But specific examples should be provided, referring to hiring practices, training, or compensation systems. Comment on the degree to which the design and implementation are strategy specific. Rely on the statement of the firm's strategy offered in exercise 1.2.

Facilitator's Note

Focus the discussion on specific examples. Make sure that participants assess human resource management practices in terms of the execution of the firm's strategy. If the participants are unable to agree that these practices are strategy specific, discuss the implications.

EXERCISE 1.4 (PAGE 31)

Leadership

Evaluate the leadership in your organization, Gibsonville, or some other firm. Be sure to use *The Cycle of Success* as the basis for making the evaluation.

Facilitator's Note

Do not allow for chronic complaining or unsubstantiated argumentation. Make sure that the evaluations are offered through the lens of *The Cycle of Success.*

GREGORY'S RETIREMENT HOME SERVICES: EXERCISE 1 (PAGE 33)

The initial replies to this case may be changed as the reader progresses through the book. But to get started it is useful to identify a set of personal services that Gregory might offer to residents, perhaps to include grocery shopping, interior cleaning, and local transportation. Be creative. Draft the value proposition for the firm.

Estimate the percentage of residents who will purchase each service, the frequency of their repeat purchases, and the price of each service. Calculate gross revenues for each of the first five years of operations. Costs and net revenues are estimated after chapters 3 and 4.

The Cycle of Success should be interpreted for Gregory. What are the implications of the model for the design of Gregory's business?

Chapter 2

EXERCISE 2.1 (PAGE 43)

Value Proposition

Complete the weighted value proposition by applying the general format of table 2.3 and using a recipe-based list (see table 2.2). Assign the relative weights as you interpret the actions of the firm. The relevant actions of the firm include the time and attention given to particular issues and to budget and personnel allocations. Also, rate the firm's performance in the execution of each aspect of the value proposition.

Facilitator's Note

This question provides rich opportunities for discussion. Individuals will find it difficult to estimate the firm's weighted value proposition. But force the process. Try to determine if their difficulties are attributable to a lack of clarity in the firm's operations. If so, push this discussion and have the participants consider how the firm can clearly express its competitive strategy. If participants offer very diverse replies, discuss how these differences could have emerged over time and ask them to consider the implications of the differences of opinion. Discuss the performance ratings offered by the participants in column 3 and determine the commonality of their views. Observed differences in the ratings should be discussed. Finally, discuss the nature of the situational leadership needed to gain greater consensus among employees.

EXERCISE 2.2 (PAGE 47)

Strategy Shift at Gibsonville

Diagnose the strategy shift at Gibsonville in terms of the Goods versus Services Continuum (see figure 2.2) by applying the characteristics of services (see pages 44–6). Consider the implications of becoming more service-like on each of the identified operating areas. Be specific about necessary changes in operations and/or policies.

Facilitator's Note

Make certain that the participants see the goods-like and the service-like aspects of their firms and their individual work. Discuss how these qualities of goods and services should influence the design of the operations, policies, and management of a firm's human resources.

EXERCISE 2.3 (PAGE 49)

Value Proposition

Use the weighted value proposition developed in exercise 2.1. Identify performance measurements that reflect the execution of the strategy. Each measurement must be quantifiable. In turn, cite operating decisions—staff size, training, equipment purchases—that can affect the performance measure.

Facilitator's Note

Review (from exercise 1.1) the recorded disagreements over the definition of Type I Buyers. Make sure that the participants agree on the definition of Type I Buyers, the weighted value proposition (exercise 2.1), and a complete set of performance measurements. Distinguish between those measures that reflect the execution of the value proposition and those that are outcomes, referring to table 2.4 (page 48). Finally, allow the participants to discuss the multiple ways in which a performance measurement can be affected.

GREGORY'S RETIREMENT HOME SERVICES: EXERCISE 2 (PAGE 50)

Review and revise (as needed) the list of services to be offered and draft the weighted value proposition. Make a qualitative assessment of the value offered to buyers and translate it to a price list. As needed, revise the gross revenue forecasts from chapter 1. Using the value proposition, define performance measurements and revisit the definition of Type I Buyers. How is Gregory to earn the trust, cooperation, and loyalty of his employees? Buyers?

Chapter 3

EXERCISE 3.1 (PAGE 56)

Mission Statements

For any firm, examine the mission statement and apply the evaluative criteria stated in table 3.3. Is the statement buyer centered? Can it be unambiguously operationalized? Does it translate into a competitive strategy? If not, make specific editorial recommendations to revise the mission statement.

Facilitator's Note

Engage the participants in discussion of the firm's mission statement, asking each individual the following: "How does the mission statement actually affect your job on a daily basis? Does the mission statement translate to a means for the firm to capture a competitive advantage over rivals?" If individuals cannot make the connection from the mission statement to their responsibilities, ask why. If individuals operationalize the mission statement in conflicting ways, ask them to determine the cause and the consequences of the differences.

EXERCISE 3.2 (PAGE 61)

Internal Assessment

To the best of your knowledge, identify the resource needs to implement the firm's value proposition. As necessary, limit your reply to the needs within your specific area of operation but be specific. In column 2, assess the firm's resource base (in your area of operation) relative to the strategy. In column 3, complete the assessment relative to the firm's closest rivals. If you lack the knowledge of another firm's capability, simply leave the space blank. Draft an Action Plan to strengthen the firm's competitive strength.

Facilitator's Note

Take full advantage of the different duties of the participants. From all participants get an assessment of the resources in their areas relative to the strategy. See if there is a consensus that they have access to the tools, knowledge, and budgets to do the job. If not, have them determine the specific items that are deficient. Make sure that each request can be defended through the weighted value proposition. Within the limits of available information, solicit their assessments of the firm's strengths relative to those of rivals. If information is lacking, discuss the importance of competitor intelligence. Make sure that the Action Plan is specific and reasonable.

EXERCISE 3.3 (PAGE 68)

Corporate-Level Strategy

If your firm engages in multiple product lines or business units, use table 3.6 to categorize the corporate-level strategy. It is possible for a firm to be engaged in more than one corporate strategy at the same time. For example, a firm engaged in leveraged relationships may also gain hygienic benefits. Develop an Action Plan to capture greater benefits from its variety of products. Use tables 3.7, 3.8, 3.9, and 3.10 to develop performance measurements.

Facilitator's Note

Be sure that the participants are able to explain the firm's corporate-level strategy. Have the participants identify performance measurements. If there is no consensus about the firm's corporate strategy, try to determine the reasons. Make sure that the Action Plan is specific and focused on the improved execution of the corporate-level strategy.

GREGORY'S RETIREMENT HOME SERVICES: EXERCISE 3 (PAGE 69)

Draft a mission statement for Gregory, making sure that the evaluative principles of table 3.3 are applied. Define and evaluate Gregory's current and (possible) future competition as well as other forces that might affect the market. How can Gregory take advantage of foreseeable changes in the market?

Given your list of services to be offered and Gregory's competitive strategy, identify the requisite tools, equipment, and systems. Be specific because this information will be used to estimate Gregory's costs. Assume a reasonable life expectancy for capital goods and apply a straight-line depreciation schedule. Are you proposing high-volume, low-margin services or low-volume, high-margin services? What are the implications for the firm's operations?

If you recommend a diverse set of services to Gregory, identify the corporate-level strategy and performance measurements.

Chapter 4

EXERCISE 4.1 (PAGE 76)

Strategy and Operations

Revisit your replies to exercises 1.2 and 3.2. Make changes as appropriate. Then, for your area of operation, identify specific tasks and functions. Evaluate their fit with respect to the requisites of implementing the firm's strategy. If the fit is weak, propose actions to improve the alignment with the firm's strategy.

Facilitator's Note

Do not allow participants to simply describe their tasks. Make sure that the participants examine their responsibilities within a strategy-specific context. If participants are unable to determine the strategy-specific nature of their duties, determine why. Is the firm's strategy poorly defined? Or have individuals failed to connect their obligations to the firm's strategy?

EXERCISE 4.2 (PAGE 81)

Internal Linkages

From the perspective of your area of operations, identify several department or operating areas on which you are dependent for parts, information, or support. Be specific about your department's needs and define a "successful delivery" from a supplying department. Be sure that the particular needs of your area are expressed in a strategy-specific manner.

Repeat this exercise from the perspective of your area's responsibility for fulfilling the needs of a receiving department. Be specific in terms of a successful delivery. Be sure that the particular needs are expressed in a strategy-specific manner.

Facilitator's Note

Insist on a specific definition of a "successful delivery," relying on the strategy-specific needs of the receiving department. Make sure that the participants do not simply describe their daily tasks.

EXERCISE 4.3 (PAGE 85)

Corporate-Level Strategy

Refer to your interpretation of the firm's corporate-level strategy in exercise 3.3. You may revise the prior answer. From your area of responsibility, describe the inter-departmental cooperation needed to implement corporate-level strategy. As appropriate, develop an Action Plan to improve that coordination and carefully assign responsibilities.

Facilitator's Note

Be sure that all participants see their roles in conducting the firm's corporate-level strategy and that each understands the requisites of coordinating the operating areas.

GREGORY'S RETIREMENT HOME SERVICES: EXERCISE 4 (PAGE 85)

Given the list of personal services to be sold, identify specific operations that must be conducted. Provide only a few examples but be specific. Also, consider the requisite linkages between operations, again noting the importance of being specific.

From these descriptions, revisit your analysis of Gregory's costs (see chapter 3). Briefly consider the organizational structure at Gregory's. Do not just draw an organizational chart; think in terms of cross-functional teams. Advise Gregory on a committee structure. For at least one committee, identify the membership by position/title.

Chapter 5

EXERCISE 5.1 (PAGE 89)

Personal Development

Identify a position to which you aspire and denote the skills and attributes needed to be successful. The position identified should be within your current firm. Express the skills and attributes in terms of the firm's strategy. Identify ways in which each of those skills and attributes can be measured, assess your current capabilities, and develop an Action Plan to improve those capabilities.

Facilitator's Note

Push each participant to go beyond technical skills and credentials and make sure that a strategy-specific approach is followed. Also, make sure that each participant defines quantifiable performance measurements for each skill and attribute. Encourage participants to extend their replies in column 1 to a timeline, with definitive checkpoints, to help them monitor their own professional development.

EXERCISE 5.2 (PAGE 93)

Mid-Level Managing

From your own experiences, describe the "up," "down," and "across" management challenges within the organization. Provide at least one specific example in each relationship. Describe the mid-manager's strategic leadership responsibilities.

Facilitator's Note

Push participants to describe their mid-level managing responsibilities within the context of *The Cycle of Success*. Make sure that all understand their own mid-manager duties.

EXERCISE 5.3 (PAGE 96)

Hiring

The table refers to a position for which you participate in the hiring. As previously completed in exercise 2.1, identify the firm's value proposition. For the specific position, identify the requisite skills and attributes and designate their relative importance. In turn, identify ways in which a candidate's capabilities can be assessed. The final two columns are not to be completed; these steps would occur only with reference to an actual résumé screening or interview.

Facilitator's Note

The challenge is to define the contribution of the position to the execution of the firm's value proposition. Be sure that participants describe the sought after skills and attributes and how each can be measured.

EXERCISE 5.4 (PAGE 97)

Reward Systems

For a position immediately below yours, describe its contributions to the execution of the firm's value proposition. In turn, build a detailed compensation plan for the award of merit pay increases or the award of an annual bonus.

Facilitator's Note

Make sure that the participants connect the criteria for the rewards with the firm's value proposition. Push the participants to describe the manner in which the system is communicated, the variables measured, and the rewards distributed. Have the participants discuss the manner in which the compensation system is announced to employees and how it is to be implemented.

EXERCISE 5.5 (PAGE 100)

Corporate-Level Strategy

Using the description of the firm's corporate-level strategy offered in exercise 3.3, identify the particular skills you need to make effective contributions.

Facilitator's Note

Make sure that all the participants understand the firm's corporate-level strategy and can describe the manner in which that strategy affects their responsibilities.

GREGORY'S RETIREMENT HOME SERVICES: EXERCISE 5 (PAGE 101)

For any position in the firm, build a hiring grid. In turn, identify a system for rewarding performance. Use this opportunity to return to your chapter 3 and 4 replies. Reconsider—as needed—the necessary size of the staff and the associated personnel costs. Be sure that you have linked the estimated number of services to be performed to the number of personnel needed by position with a reasonable assessment of productivity.

Chapter 6

EXERCISE 6.1 (PAGE 107)

Performance Measurements

Using the value proposition developed in exercise 2.1, establish a set of performance measurements. Revisions to the exercise 2.1 reply are fully acceptable. Carefully distinguish between those measurements that reflect the execution of the value proposition from those that are financial outcomes. Set performance targets (make assumptions and use judgment) for each of the measurements.

Facilitator's Note

Initially, all participants should develop on their own a set of performance measures. Discussion should take place only after each participant has completed a list. During discussion, be sure that the set of performance measurements provides guidance for all operating areas; be sure that the measurements reflect the execution of the firm's value proposition; and be sure that the participants distinguish between execution of the value proposition and the financial achievements of the firm.

If disagreements exist, discuss them and consider the implications. Disagreements over the performance measures must be settled because the reading/discussion is nearing completion. Do not accept an agreement by default or convenience. Rather, the performance measures must be acknowledged as the proper expression of the firm's strategy.

EXERCISE 6.2 (PAGE 114)

Corporate-Level Strategy

Revisit your prior statements about the firm's corporate-level strategy (exercise 3.3). Make changes as appropriate. Identify measurements that reflect the execution of the firm's corporate strategy.

Facilitator's Note

Make sure that the participants have developed an appropriate set of performance measures. Discuss the manner in which the firm can improve the execution of its corporate strategy.

GREGORY'S RETIREMENT HOME SERVICES: EXERCISE 6 (PAGE 114)

Build a set of performance measurements for Gregory. Using your best judgment, establish target values for at least some of the measurements. For example, if speed of service matters, define the target speed in hours or minutes. Then, review the prior estimates of staff size and equipment to determine if those projections are sensible within the context of the number of services expected to be sold, the target performance levels, and reasonable estimates of productivity.

Keep in mind that Gregory can expect to be invited to expand his business to other retirement communities if this initial venture raises the quality of life (and property values) of the current residents. Hence, the target values should conform to these long-run aspirations.

Chapter 7

EXERCISE 7.1 (PAGE 118)

Management and Leadership

Reply to the sixteen questions. Given the distinctions between management and strategic leadership, evaluate your skills. Propose a personal action to strengthen your strategic leadership skills.

Facilitator's Note

Use the distinctions between management and leadership to encourage introspection. Have the participants offer examples from their own experiences.

EXERCISE 7.2 (PAGE 120)

Leadership

Parts A and B call for you to diagnose the commonality of view of your firm's competitive strategy and to propose a situational leadership style. In part C, write a detailed memo to Ted Barker Jr. as if you were a consultant to the firm.

Facilitator's Note

Allow the participants to discuss concepts of situational leadership. Make sure that their action plans are sound, sensible, and operational.

GREGORY'S RETIREMENT HOME SERVICES: EXERCISE 7 (PAGE 121)

Prepare a thorough report for Gregory. Use your replies to the previous exercises, though changes are acceptable. The end product should include a five-year spreadsheet of projected revenues and costs. The costs should be estimated as a result of the requirements to execute the firm's value proposition and the target values for the performance measurements. The revenues should be associated with the value proposition, the rate of market penetration, pricing, and repeat purchase presumptions. Describe the firm's internal operations. Describe the risks and rewards to Gregory. Make a recommendation to him. Should he invest in this business?

Index

activities, 20, 22

Balanced Scorecard, 48
benchmarking, 23–24
best practices, 23
buyer loyalty, 22, 26–27

coaching, 96
communications, 105, 117–21
compensation systems, 20, 27, 95
competitive strategy: advantage, 17–18, 24; explicit, 57–58; reasonable, 59; relative analysis, 55–56, 59–61; strength of, 18–19, 57
competitive theme, 44, 71, 73
conglomerate relationships, 65, 83, 99, 112
corporate level strategies, 65–68, 83–84, 99–100, 111–13
cost of acquisition, 39–40, 110
cost of new buyers, 19–20
cross selling, 46, 47, 113
The Cycle of Success, 16–30, 115–21

decision making. *See* strategy specific decisions

employee loyalty, 22
empowerment, 44
external analysis, 62

financial performance, 105, 106
flow of work, 80

Gibsonville Lantern Company, 9–12
goods vs. services, 44–46
Gregory's Retirement Home Services: case, 32–33; exercises, 33, 50, 69, 85, 101, 114, 121

hiring practices, 72–73, 95
holistic analysis, 75, 77
hygienic relationships, 66, 84, 99, 112

integrated activities, 29
internal assessments, 59–60
internal service map, 79

leadership. *See* strategic leadership
leveraged relationships, 67, 84, 100, 112
linkages, 22–23, 79–82, 88, 91
listening, 98

macroeconomics, 62–63
management by theme, 23, 98, 113
mentoring, 96
microeconomics, 63–64
mid-level management, 77–78, 92–94
mission statements, 53–56
motivation, 90, 94

nagging, 28, 96

operations, strategy specific, 19, 20, 72
organizational culture, 29, 94–95, 116
organizational structure, 22, 80, 98

performance measures: corporate level, 112; departmental, 109; elasticity, 108–10; financial, 105; firm, 46–48, 104, 109; individual, 49–50; management by, 103–5
policies and procedures, 27, 55, 72–77
Porter, Michael, 20, 71
postassessments, 125–27
preassessments, 5–8
price, 38–40
process quality, 37–38

Quality Buyer Ratio, 20
quotas, 72

results, 36–37

situational leadership, 29–30, 119
skills and attributes, 26–27, 88
straddling, 22

strategic group map, 64
strategic leadership, 31, 35, 76, 87, 90–94, 116–18
strategy and mission, 27, 53, 56–58
strategy specific decisions, 22, 24, 78, 80
superior performance, 16, 30

teaching role, 31, 117
teams, 22, 80, 82
tools and equipment, 28, 60
training, 75, 97
Type I Buyers, 19, 25, 59, 110

value proposition: articulation of, 105; buyer's, 36, 42, 110; equation, 17–18, 57; execution of, 20; recipe-based, 41; rigidity, 21–22; seller's, 18, 38, 42, 76, 110; target values, 106–8; theme-based, 41
visionary, 31

About the Author

Dr. William G. Forgang is professor of economics and business at Mount Saint Mary's College in Emmitsburg, Maryland. In addition, he maintains an active consulting schedule specializing in the areas of business planning, competitive strategy, and staff development.